About the Author

HARRY SHUTT was educated at Oxford and Warwick universities. He worked for six years in the Development and Planning Division of the Economist Intelligence Unit (EIU). He then moved to the Research Department of the General and Municipal Workers' Union (1973–76) and subsequently became Chief Economist at the Fund for Research and Investment for the Development of Africa (1977–79). Since then he has been an independent economic consultant.

His previous books include *The Myth of Free Trade: Patterns of Protectionism since 1945* (Basil Blackwell/The Economist, 1985); *The Trouble with Capitalism: An Inquiry into the Causes of Global Economic Failure* (Zed Books, 1998); *A New Democracy: Alternatives to a Bankrupt World Order* (Zed Books, 2001).

The Decline of Capitalism

Can a Self-Regulated Profits System Survive?

———————

HARRY SHUTT

SIRD
Kuala Lumpur

David Philip
Cape Town

ZED BOOKS
London & New York

The Decline of Capitalism was first published in 2005 by

In Malaysia: Strategic Information Research Development (SIRD),
No. 11/4E, Petaling Jaya, 46200 Selangor

In Southern Africa: David Philip Publishers (Pty Ltd),
99 Garfield Road, Claremont 7700, South Africa

In the rest of the world: Zed Books Ltd,
7 Cynthia Street, London N1 9JF, UK, and
Room 400, 175 Fifth Avenue, New York, NY 10010, USA

www.zedbooks.co.uk

Designed and typeset in Monotype Jansen by Illuminati, Grosmont
Cover designed by Andrew Corbett
Printed and bound in the EU by Cox & Wyman, Reading

Distributed in the USA exclusively by Palgrave, a division of
St Martin's Press, LLC, 175 Fifth Avenue, New York, NY 10010

A catalogue record for this book is available from the British Library
Library of Congress Cataloging-in-Publication Data available

ISBN 1 84277 400 X (Hb)
ISBN 1 84277 401 8 (Pb)

ISBN 983 2535 53 0 Pb (Malaysia)

Contents

Introduction:

Millennium Meltdown

For many in the Western world who lived through the last two decades of the twentieth century, the intensity of the global financial crisis that has been manifest since the start of the new century is inevitably hard to come to terms with. For since about 1980 a strident consensus has developed in the political main-stream on the enormous benefits that would flow from the eco-nomic liberalisation undertaken both within and between the vast majority of countries all over the world in that time. Such a movement to decontrol markets, it has been claimed, would act as an antidote to the excessive regulation and state involvement in the economy which were alleged to have caused the economic slowdown of the 1970s.

This belief that the spread of 'free markets' would lead to general prosperity was clearly reinforced by the spectacular col-lapse, at the end of the 1980s, of the Soviet Union – dedicated to centralised planning and state ownership – amid manifest eco-nomic failure. The vision of a brave new liberalised world was made all the more seductive by the associated notion of global-isation, in which not only were barriers to trade and financial flows to be swept away but a cornucopia of new market and wealth-creating opportunities would be created by advances in electronics and cybertechnology.

Yet in contrast to this euphoric prospectus depicted by official propaganda a very different global reality has been unfolding in the transition from the twentieth to the twenty-first century. Instead of indications of rising prosperity the world has witnessed increasing economic dysfunction and deteriorating prospects for most of its people. The main symptoms of this systemic failure have been

- Deepening economic stagnation. Instead of the promised revival of economic growth from the levels of the 1970s the rate of increase in global output (as reflected in average GDP growth) has continued to decline in each succeeding decade.
- Growing economic insecurity within the rich countries of the industrialised West (including Japan). This has condemned a substantial minority – amounting in countries such as Britain and the United States to 30 per cent or more of the population – to the status of a seemingly permanent 'underclass' of those living in poverty. Since the turn of the century, moreover, the spreading failure of private pension schemes in the wake of the stock market collapse has raised the spectre of poverty or destitution in old age for many more who have hitherto been able to regard themselves as comfortably off.
- Increasing marginalisation of the poor countries. The plight of the 80 per cent of the world's population who live in the 'developing' world and in the impoverished countries of the former Soviet bloc – where living standards have always been a mere fraction of those in the industrialised world – has gone from bad to worse. While this reality is not necessarily reflected in official statistics of average income (which conceal

the grotesque disparities between rich and poor within these countries), it is unmistakably clear from the rising numbers of economic migrants fleeing these countries, the spreading incidence of state bankruptcy and the collapse of law and order – leading, in more and more cases, to outright civil war.

- Ever more frequent crises in liberalised financial markets – often linked to a growing incidence of fraud and corporate criminality – which are both cause and effect of deepening economic stagnation and insecurity.

Yet these signs of intensifying malaise have long been concealed by what is evidently a concerted campaign of misinformation and outright denial orchestrated by what we may conveniently term 'the global establishment' – that is, those vested interests that effectively dominate public opinion through political parties and the mass media. The extreme nature of this official refusal to confront reality – a phenomenon which will be a recurrent theme of this book – is nowhere more striking than in the general denial that there has been any long-term slowdown in economic growth since the 1970s. The author has been made keenly aware of this tendency by a distinguished reviewer of his earlier work *The Trouble with Capitalism*, who asserted that the book provides no evidence for the existence of chronic economic stagnation – even though it actually includes a chart (based on OECD data) demonstrating the decade-by-decade decline in GDP growth rates.[1]

By such Orwellian processes of deception the establishment has until recently been able to divert attention from the reality of deepening economic crisis and systemic dysfunction across developed and developing worlds alike. Distraction from these ills has been sought in successive propaganda campaigns emphasising the positive. A favourite ploy in this continuing effort has been to exalt the supposed success of economies which could be depicted as offering a model to be emulated by the underachieving remainder – from Japan in the 1980s to Mexico and the East Asian 'tigers' in the 1990s. By 1998, however, successive financial crises had largely destroyed belief in these supposed success stories, whose short-lived advantage had in any case owed less to liberalisation and far more to state intervention and officially sponsored market distortion than their neoliberal cheerleaders in the West were willing to allow.[2]

Before the end of the century, therefore, the prophets of capitalist triumphalism had been reduced to proclaiming the United States as the new beacon of economic hope – even though its economy had often been portrayed in the 1970s and 1980s as a sclerotic failure compared with ascendant Japan. By the late 1990s it was depicted as having been reborn on a wave of entrepreneurial dynamism unleashed by unprecedented technological advances in electronics and telecommunications – the so-called new economy. Yet scarcely had the tumult of millennium fireworks died away in 2000 than the supposed wonders of America's 'new economy' were shown to be a mirage – one, moreover, whose image of success was soon to be revealed as built on phantom output data and false accounting on an unprecedented scale.

The lies and financial crimes that have underpinned this evanescent economic 'miracle' are only now being exposed as a result of a financial crisis which, it is already clear, is the most catastrophic to hit the world since that of 1929–31, which heralded the Depression of the 1930s. Writing in the midst of this unfolding disaster, it may seem premature to assess its full extent or significance. This may appear all the more problematic now that the US authorities, in conjunction with leading private financial institutions, have succeeded in engineering a rally in the markets (since March 2003) which is claimed to be the start of a global economic revival – even though stock market valuations are again almost as excessive (relative to earnings) as they were on the eve of the crash in 2000. It is nevertheless already clear that the crisis is confronting the people of the developed world in particular with the prospect of sharply reduced living standards – to an extent that the majority can hardly have imagined they would ever have to face. This setback is reflected not only in restricted employment and earning opportunities for those of working age – belying official attempts to claim that there is actually a shortage of labour in Britain and other European countries – but also now in the prospect of reduced levels of social security, pensions and health care for those of all ages and in all social classes.

For the 80 per cent of the world's people living in poor countries (including most of the former Soviet bloc) the demonstrable failure of globalisation has meant a still greater increase in deprivation – and loss of hope – than that experienced in the industrialised world. In perhaps the most spectacular instance of failure, Argentina – hitherto one of the richest countries in Latin America and lauded in the 1990s as one of the most successful exponents of 'neoliberalism' – has since suffered a financial collapse that has pushed almost 60 per cent of its people below the poverty line. Less publicised are the sufferings of most of the people of China, now hailed as the great economic hope of the new liberalised world – despite being still an authoritarian Communist dictatorship – because of its continuing reported growth rates of 7–9 per cent a year. Yet in rural areas (where the vast majority of the country's 1.2 billion population still live) the World Bank has reported a dramatic deterioration in health-care provision as the resources devoted to it have been curtailed in parallel with moves towards a more market-oriented economy favouring urban areas. As a result by 1998 average expenditure on rural health care was less than half that in urban areas and in many poor counties public provision had virtually collapsed.[3] This in turn is reflected in a rise in the incidence of tuberculosis to 40–50 per cent of the population in some areas and a catastrophic epidemic of HIV/AIDS, realities which the government has tried at once to ignore and to hide from the world.

Seen against the background of such developments, the crisis that has erupted since the stock market crash of 2000 should hardly have come as a surprise – except to those totally bamboozled by the combined effects of official misinformation and financial fraud. At all events it is now obvious that the meltdown of financial markets itself constitutes an additional adverse economic factor of momentous importance. This is underlined by the widely accepted parallel between the present financial crisis and that which followed the Wall Street crash of 1929.

For even if the widespread banking failures induced by the earlier crash have not yet been experienced in the present one, it is already apparent that the numbers of people set to suffer serious hardship as a direct result of the 2000 crash are much greater than seventy years earlier, particularly in the Anglo-Saxon countries. This is because, in contrast to the position in 1929–31, the fortunes of hundreds of millions of ordinary people are today directly linked to movements in the securities markets thanks to the vastly greater scale of institutional funds invested in the market. These institutions (comprising pension funds, mutual funds and unit trusts) are vehicles for investing the savings and pension contributions of workers in securities with a view to providing them with an adequate income in retirement. As has long been predicted, however, the attraction and viability of such funds have been quite unable to withstand a deep and sustained downturn in securities markets which was bound to undermine their value and – in the case of funds committed to providing guaranteed levels of pension – their solvency.

Yet even as the scale of the unfolding financial debacle is becoming inescapably obvious, there is no public recognition on the part of mainstream political parties or organs of opinion in the Western world of any of the fundamental weaknesses of the existing model of economic organisation. The reason for this failure to confront the reality of economic failure is not, it should be clear, an inability on the part of world leaders to understand the true nature of the underlying problem. Rather it is because any open recognition of reality would lead to the inescapable conclusion that

- the dominant capitalist system based on the primacy of private profit is by now not only as unstable and destructive as ever but hopelessly outmoded in relation to modern economic needs and technological developments, and that
- a more functional alternative would inevitably entail phasing out the wasteful diversion of economic value added into the pockets of the small minority who also (through their disproportionate wealth) exercise largely unaccountable political power.

The tragic irony is that, for all its pretensions to be a beacon of democracy, the West is thus demonstrating that its political structures are no more capable of coming to terms with inevitable change than was the Soviet Union prior to the advent of Mikhail Gorbachev. Moreover, it is becoming distressingly clear that the governments of what are supposed to be the world's most advanced countries are now so permeated with corrupt and criminal elements as seemingly to have lost any sense of responsibility for the public interest at all.

This prevalence of unreason and betrayal in the face of such global catastrophe is obviously a cause for deep pessimism. For it is all too easy to believe that the predominant response to such manifest failure of the existing order will be one of violence and repression rather than a rational search for a more humane alternative. It is against this background that the present work seeks to offer a reasoned explanation of how the world has descended into such economic chaos, recognising that virtually none of the analysis presented to the public through the media is free of the self-serving propaganda of the ruling vested interests.

The book has been conceived as a sequel to the author's earlier work, *The Trouble with Capitalism*,[4] first published in 1998. In view of the upheavals that have shaken the global economy in the intervening six years it seems desirable to revisit and update that analysis, although readers familiar with it may well think it has been substantially validated by events. For the sake of coherence some repetition of the arguments of the previous work has naturally been unavoidable (particularly in the first three chapters), although an effort has been made, as far as possible, to present them in concise form, supplemented with cross-references to the earlier work where appropriate. It is also hoped that the emphasis on brevity will enhance the book's accessibility to a wider audience. Thus the text seeks to tread a fine line between the twin dangers of tedium and lack of clarity. The attempt will have been justified if it succeeds in helping more people not only to see through the mendacious propaganda of the global establishment but to focus their minds on seeking radical alternatives to the manifestly exhausted profits system.

I

The Long Road to Disaster

The tensions that have produced the present world financial crisis may be seen as largely endemic in the Western world since capitalism first became the dominant form of economic organisation in Europe at the time of the Industrial Revolution some two hundred years ago. The particular feature of the system that has caused most concern and distress throughout this time has been the very strong cyclical fluctuations it has produced in markets – leading to alternate boom and bust. It is true that this was by no means a completely new phenomenon in economic history, in that market cycles had always been a feature of sectors such as agriculture even in the pre-capitalist era. What was new under capitalism, however, was that the pressure to maximise profits in the interests of shareholders and financiers meant that employers felt far stronger pressure than under the previous more or less feudal economy to cut costs during a downturn by laying off workers – or at least cutting their wages. Because of such pressures the sharp reduction of wages across the economy as a whole acted to intensify the decline in demand for goods and services and thus prolong the downward phase of the cycle.

Taming the business cycle

The disastrous social consequences of the resulting periodic depressions in economic activity caused by this 'business cycle' were first demonstrated across Europe as a whole in the 1840s. This gave rise to such widespread misery that it provoked revolutionary upheavals in almost every continental country in 1848, which was also the year when the *Communist Manifesto* of Marx and Engels first appeared. Even though this ferment left the existing political order substantially intact, it had a lasting impact in advancing recognition of the rights and needs of the mass of workers who had hitherto been almost completely marginalised, politically as well as economically. Hence already by the late nineteenth century a number of 'bourgeois' states of Western Europe had felt constrained not only to extend voting rights to a steadily increasing proportion of the population, but to provide minimal social protection and services for the working masses (including old-age pensions, unemployment insurance and elementary education).

If the need for basic social security was generally accepted in the industrialised world by the end of World War I – though conspicuously not in the United States – such defence mechanisms were to prove woefully inadequate in face of the next great cyclical economic collapse. This event – the Depression of the 1930s, precipitated by the Wall Street Crash of 1929–31 – was still more catastrophic in its consequences than the disaster of the 1840s. This was because it produced not only a tidal wave of financial failure and corporate collapse (so typical of earlier depressions); it also demonstrated the inability of the rudimentary social welfare systems then in place to protect the vast numbers of newly unemployed from the ravages of a major cyclical downturn. This was because it had never been envisaged that the system would be called on to provide protection for such vast numbers of unemployed as were created by the global collapse of economic activity that occurred in the early 1930s. Faced with such a disaster – and restricted by the demands of traditional financial orthodoxy that a more or less balanced budget be maintained – governments such as Britain's then Labour administration felt they had no choice but to cut benefit levels. The political consequences of this trauma – in a world where the working masses had acquired much greater rights and expectations than a hundred years earlier – were dramatic, particularly in continental Europe. Indeed it is hard to dispute that this economic catastrophe was probably the single most decisive factor leading to World War II, the most destructive conflict in history.

Hence by the end of the war it was generally recognised throughout the industrialised world that economic management largely wedded to the principles of financial orthodoxy and laissez-faire had proved inadequate and unacceptable. It was therefore decreed more or less everywhere that government policy must henceforth give priority to assuring high levels of employment, if necessary intervening to sustain the level of economic activity through higher levels of government spending and deficits – in line with the precepts of the economist J.M. Keynes.[1] As a complement to such macroeconomic strategies it was also accepted that social welfare programmes should provide comprehensive benefits to ensure that those who did lose their jobs would have a decent basic standard of living. In fact it was part of the rationale of Keynesian economics that the increase in public welfare expenditure occasioned by any cyclical downturn in economic activity would act as an 'automatic stabiliser' by sustaining the level of consumer demand in circumstances where it would otherwise fall, thus helping to avert or limit the classic downward spiral of economic activity.

While such were the bare bones of Keynesian economic strategy, it is important to note that it became linked to a broader ideology of what was known as the 'mixed economy', in which state intervention in and interaction with the private sector were recognised as necessary and desirable. The essential nature of this relationship was that the state would provide selective support for investment and production by private enterprise, through various forms of subsidy or protection, on the basis that this would be conducive to sustaining the levels of economic activity and employment by now regarded as 'public goods' – that is, key objectives of official policy. Yet it is also important to recall that the achievement of such macroeconomic goals was never viewed in terms of precise targets or detailed planning of inputs and outputs, as under the Soviet system of economic management. Rather it was to be based on the very Keynesian concept of 'pump priming', whereby injections of public money into the economy would both stimulate demand and boost the 'animal spirits' of private entrepreneurs, whose confidence was sustained by the belief that the government had an interest in ensuring their success.

Likewise, for the most part there was no formal compact between the state and private corporations concerning the levels of investment, output or employment to be assured as a trade-off for public support, with such decisions being left largely at the discretion of management, particularly in the Anglo-Saxon countries.[2] Indeed the weight of opinion, as generally reflected in the mainstream political parties and media, was that the aim of optimising economic performance was best served by keeping official interference in the management of the private sector to a minimum and trusting the latter to protect the public interest through 'self-regulation'. Such, for example, was the typical response of business to successive attempts in Britain and elsewhere to impose controls on prices and incomes in the 1960s and 1970s.

This attitude was often justified by assertions that such controls amounted to an unwarranted distortion of market forces, cheerfully ignoring the extent to which market forces were already being systematically distorted in favour of business interests by official support and subsidies of all kinds.

Post-war delusions

Whatever may be seen with hindsight as the inherent contradictions of the Keynesian corporatist model, it cannot be denied that it held largely undisputed sway among Western economic policymakers for a generation after World War II. Its sustained popularity during this period is not hard to explain. For it coincided with a period of worldwide economic expansion without precedent in the capitalist era, as output (gross domestic product) rose by an average of 4.3 per cent a year in the industrialised (OECD) countries between 1950 and 1973 – compared with a historic average of only around half that level. Given that this record performance was achieved in a period when an evidently revolutionary form of economic management was being applied, it is entirely understandable that economists and non-economists alike should have concluded that this was more than a coincidence. Indeed it was widely believed that the Holy Grail of capitalist economics – the secret of how to assure perpetual growth – had finally been discovered.

Yet by the early 1970s there were already signs that this comforting belief was becoming untenable. This was indicated by the fact that it was getting harder to maintain high growth rates by applying the Keynesian tools of demand management (fiscal and monetary policy) in the industrialised countries. For it had only proved possible to sustain relatively rapid growth by relaxing fiscal discipline to the point where budget deficits became the rule rather the exception and by keeping monetary policy lax enough to risk growing indiscipline among both lenders and borrowers. The inevitable result, in conditions of continuing more or less full employment and high levels of capacity utilisation, was a steady rise in OECD rates of inflation from around 3 per cent in the mid-1960s to the wholly unsustainable average level of 8 per cent in 1973.

The effect of this inflationary bubble was to precipitate a financial crisis at the end of 1973, which paved the way for the recession of 1974–75 – the first year-on-year fall in output in the industrialised world since World War II. The scapegoats generally identified at the time as responsible for this upset to the comfortable Keynesian consensus ranged from the Organisation of Petroleum Exporting Countries (OPEC) – whose decision in October 1973 to raise the crude oil price fourfold undoubtedly triggered the financial crisis – to the allegedly excessive demands of trade unions for wage increases.

What seemingly no economist managed to grasp was the possibility that the real lesson of the crisis, in relation to the historic pattern of the capitalist business cycle, was that nothing had fundamentally changed, and that the inherent limits to the rate of economic growth were as real as ever. Given that the first symptom of the crisis was inflation – which economists had all been trained to regard as an indicator of excessively rapid demand growth – their failure to recognise it as a portent of declining growth was perhaps forgivable. On the other hand the persistence of high inflation through the recession of 1974–75 (a phenomenon known as stagflation) was a mortal blow to the Keynesian belief that expansionary demand management policies – monetary or fiscal – could provide a sufficient guarantee of sustained economic growth.

Yet even if few people seemed at the time to recognise that permanently slower growth in underlying consumer demand might be limiting the rate of economic expansion, there are grounds for believing that such concerns had already begun to influence policy as early as the 1960s. Thus the relaxation in this period of restrictions on a number of areas of consumption such as gambling and pornography – although justified on libertarian grounds in what some now remember as an age of permissiveness – were doubtless more readily accepted by a political and financial establishment anxious to exploit new market opportunities.[3]

Had either the Keynesians or their opponents been concerned to identify the true causes of the 1970s' downturn, they would surely have recognised that it was indeed the result of deficient demand; or, more precisely, that the prolonged post-war boom had been fed by a level of unsatisfied demand which was wholly exceptional and unsustainable. While there may be some dispute as to precisely what made the post-war period so unusual in this regard, it seems clear that it was primarily a function of (a) the massive need for reconstruction in war-shattered Europe and Japan and (b) the huge pent-up demand for consumer goods (and services) that had arisen during the Depression years of the 1930s and the succeeding period of war-time austerity.[4]

Such a conclusion, which may seem more or less obvious with the benefit of hindsight, was naturally unpalatable for Keynesians in the 1970s – and has remained so to the diehards ever since – since it further called into question their claim to have discovered a lasting antidote to the business cycle. Instead it tended to expose them to the charge from their 'neoclassical' opponents that their policies, by distorting market forces, had promoted wasteful over-investment and misallocation of resources. Significantly, however, the neoclassical and 'monetarist' economists, whose influence became dominant from the mid-1970s, were just as reluctant to accept that the business cycle was an inescapable fact of capitalist life. Indeed, by the early 1980s they were eagerly proclaiming that by radically liberalising markets and 'rolling back the frontiers of the state' they would be able to achieve the sustained growth that had eluded the exponents of Keynesian doctrine.

The return of the business cycle and the rejection of orthodoxy

From the onset of recession in the mid-1970s there was unanimous concern on the part of the governments of the major industrialised countries to make a determined effort to shore up the world economy in such a way as to preserve the status quo broadly intact. This was reflected in the creation of the Group of Seven (G7) annual forum representing the largest industrial market economies,[5] which was set up in 1975 with the avowed purpose of coordinating global recovery from the recession that was then still afflicting it. (The fact that it has continued to meet every year since then may perhaps be seen as a telling comment on how far such a recovery has ever been achieved, on any kind of durable basis, given that recession has been a recurrent feature of the world economy ever since.)

The refusal of the global establishment at the time to contemplate the possibility that a restoration of rapid expansion might not be attainable reflects the impact of the post-war zeitgeist of perpetual growth, which left no room in the minds of policymakers for any return of the business cycle. The refusal to accept such a possibility was, moreover, all too well grounded in justified fears of possible financial meltdown at a time when the balance sheets of many banks and other institutions were replete with actual or potential bad debts. In particular it clearly called in question the sustainability of funded pension schemes, which had been established in the United States since the 1950s as the main source of retirement income for most private sector employees. For these were clearly not viable on the assumption of any prolonged stagnation or slump, which would inevitably be reflected in the value of securities underpinning the funds.

Thus when recession did strike in 1974 it was immediately clear that an old-fashioned financial bust – involving wholesale bankruptcy and write-off of assets – was not an acceptable solution. Instead the extensive resort to official bail-outs of financial institutions ensured that there were only a handful of bank failures. Likewise the US Congress enacted the Employee Retirement Income Security Act in 1974 in order to ensure state protection of private-sector funded pension schemes against insolvency.[6] In fact this little-noticed measure may be seen, if only with hindsight, as providing the crucial prop to the parasitic fund-management industry which has since grown to exert such a massive and pernicious influence over the development of latter-day global capitalism.

At the same time the establishment resorted to propagating the fantasy that sustained economic growth would revive if only short-term sacrifices were made – that is, restrictions on wage rises and welfare benefits – and strict anti-inflationary policies adopted. This inevitably entailed a tacit retreat from the post-war commitment to full employment and social equity in favour of the corporate agenda – exemplified by the savage decimation of British industrial capacity brought about by the Thatcher administration in 1980–82. But progressively, as sustained recovery proved illusory – with recession returning at the start of the 1980s – the whole strategy became less plausible. A particularly obvious symptom of its failure was that public sector deficits began to rise as a result of continuing stagnation in output growth, resulting in increased calls on public funds – not least because of higher welfare bills. This was reflected in the fact that the ratio of gross public debt to GDP in the industrialised countries more than doubled (on average) between 1974 and 1997 – to 77 per cent.

Bearing in mind the political necessity of continuing to pay lip-service to the maintenance of a high level of economic activity and employment, the general unwillingness to recognise that demand deficiency and recession were bound after all to be recurrent features of the capitalist system is scarcely surprising. For if it was conceded that the capitalist economy – whether 'mixed' or otherwise – could not deliver a minimum degree of durable income security to the mass of the population, it was not fanciful to suppose that demands for more radical approaches might prove irresistible. Moreover, it was easy to see that any such alternatives were likely to entail a greater degree of public control over the private sector and greater redistribution of income to the disadvantage of the dominant vested interests – including big business.

Yet if it was politically unacceptable to the establishment to acknowledge that the capitalist business cycle was ultimately inescapable, it was equally so from a financial perspective. For it would have meant coming to terms with the potentially massive losses that would be inflicted on investors as a necessary consequence of the devaluation of financial securities – and the assets that they represented – which must ensue from anything like the kind of shakeout of excess capacity that would occur under the normal operation of market forces. It was clear, moreover, that such a disaster could only be prevented by diverting an increasing share of stagnating or shrinking national income (economic value-added) to satisfying the inescapable demands of the owners of capital for more profits.

For these reasons the so-called neoclassical or neoliberal revolution in economic thinking of the 1980s rejected from the outset any genuine return to financial orthodoxy. Indeed, so far from following the classical dictates of sound money and balanced budgets demanded by the economic high priests of the pre-Keynesian era, the neoclassical school maintained that

- tax-cutting combined with deregulation could 'unleash the forces of enterprise' and thereby generate accelerated growth and hence (it was pretended) sufficient extra taxes to achieve long-term budgetary balance (few people noticed that this theory of 'supply-side' economics was in fact essentially Keynesian in spirit, except that its adherents were also firm believers in cutting social welfare);
- control of the money supply – principally through official manipulation of interest rates – was sufficient to keep inflation under control (the essence of the doctrine of monetarism, which the Thatcher administration initially claimed to be the basis of its economic policy).

In fact it quickly became apparent that monetarism and financial liberalisation were mutually contradictory strategies. For, by ending controls on capital movements and most restrictions on the ability of financial institutions to issue credit and different types of financial instrument, governments were effectively abandoning their control over the money supply, perhaps without even realising what they were doing.

The cancer of 'moral hazard'

Thus as the 1980s unfolded it was increasingly evident that the neoliberal ideology which was supposed to have supplanted the Keynesian model based on extensive state intervention was in fact hopelessly undermined by the private sector's incurable addiction to public subsidy and protection. Yet the dangerous implications of this reality – effectively concealed from the majority of the public by an establishment propaganda smokescreen, combined with extensive measures indicating that the frontiers of the state were indeed being rolled back – were for long scarcely recognised. For, by giving private enterprise, particularly in the financial sector, increased licence to create and allocate credit while yet maintaining an implicit or explicit guarantee that the state would underwrite any major losses, the authorities were giving a powerful incentive to irresponsible, or even criminal, behaviour. This phenomenon, referred to by the few who have been willing to recognise its existence as 'moral hazard', defines the essentially fraudulent nature of the neoliberal prospectus. For while, as noted above, the corporatist, mixed-economy model of the post-war era had always implicitly assumed a trade-off between state support for the private sector and the latter's obligation to help meet the collective economic goals of the community, the moral hazard model actually provided an incentive to anti-social conduct. Moreover, in a climate of intensifying stagnation, where corporate profitability was ever harder to sustain at minimum acceptable levels, the temptation for corporate managers not merely to allocate funds to excessively risky investment but to resort to outright fraud became increasingly irresistible.

It is thus ironic to reflect that Keynesianism, long hailed as the saviour of the capitalist system, may have turned into the key instrument of its ultimate ruin. For, by drawing private enterprise into such lasting dependence on public subsidy, it may well be judged to have set capitalism on a path of decline from which it may never be able to recover.

Liberalisation and the 'race to the bottom'

A related contradiction at the heart of the neoliberal model of capitalism has been the enforced exposure of national economies to ever more intense and unfair competition – even as the ruling elite have been allowed unparalleled indulgence in bending market forces to suit their narrow corporate interests. This has notably led to pressure on governments (including those of the poorest countries) to cut corporate tax levels severely – and even to offer tax breaks which they can ill afford – in order to attract or retain employment-creating investment. This pressure has only intensified as excess capacity has spread throughout virtually every sector of the world economy as a consequence of persistent low growth, thus making new investment opportunities extremely scarce. At the same time the process of globalisation has allowed countries that do not even pretend to (a) offer minimum levels of protection or rights to workers (in line with the conventions of the International Labour Organisation or the Universal Declaration of Human Rights), or (b) observe minimum standards of environmental protection or public health safeguards in economic sectors, to trade on equal terms with countries that do largely comply with such standards. Perhaps the most notable deviant in this regard (among many others) has been China, a country which has been allowed to capture a huge share of world markets for manufactures by breaking all the rules while nevertheless being held up as a role model by supporters of globalisation.

Inevitably this aspect of globalisation has led to a competitive lowering of taxation and other standards – commonly referred to by critics of the process as a 'race to the bottom'. It is striking that the global establishment – representing the obvious beneficiaries of this tendency (big business and the owners of capital) – has refused to recognise the ultimately unsustainable social consequences of the resulting progressive damage to public services and human welfare. Perhaps still more remarkable is their collective failure to grasp that such anomie is quite as likely to deter investment as to encourage it, given the increased threat of unfair competition that it poses to entrepreneurs – not to mention the impact of deteriorating infrastructure.

The failure of neoliberalism, 1980–2000

By the mid-1980s the combination of prolonged low growth (resulting in the creation of substantial pent-up demand during years of restrained consumption), widespread market deregulation and intensive neoliberal propaganda had created the conditions for a worldwide rebound in economic activity which was to last the rest of the decade. Even so, average GDP growth for the OECD countries in the 1984–89 period was still less than had been achieved through the 1970s, then and subsequently regarded as a decade of economic failure and stagnation. Yet the revival was enough to sustain a new bull market in equities, which had actually begun in 1982, that was to last for the next eighteen years and see an unprecedented tenfold rise in share prices.[7] Such extreme euphoria, which enabled investors to brush aside the stock market 'crash' of 1987, was nonetheless unable to conceal the underlying weakness of the real economy, which led to another inflationary bust in 1989–90 (albeit less spectacular than that of ten years earlier).

The subsequent recession exposed serious flaws in the new model of deregulated capitalism, since much of the enterprise it had unleashed, so far from providing durable growth and economic prosperity, was shown to have been based on speculative fantasy, if not outright fraud. The resulting widespread financial failures – particularly associated with real-estate speculation – thus paved the way for renewed economic stagnation in the 1990s. Nowhere was this more true than in Japan, where colossal bad debts crippled the banking system and stifled any scope for revival of activity. This was partly because restraints on enforcement of the bankruptcy laws made it difficult for lenders to foreclose on collateral, thus preventing any reduction of the huge excess capacity in many sectors and discouraging expansion by financially healthy companies. At the same time the country was no longer able, as in the 1970s and 1980s, to exploit an undervalued yen to gain an ever rising share of export markets. Thus while the rest of the industrialised world was able, as the 1990s wore on, to struggle back to growth rates that were at least no lower than they had achieved in the previous decade, Japanese business remained largely hamstrung and its economy mired in a recession from which it shows no sign of emerging.

While Western commentators were at first hard put to explain this singular failure of what had until recently been hailed as a world economic superpower, they soon fell to ascribing it to peculiar rigidities and imbalances in the Japanese system which they had somehow previously overlooked. Yet they studiously ignored the reality that the rest of the industrialised world was only able to avoid the paralysis afflicting Japan thanks to much greater willingness to subsidise and recapitalise largely insolvent institutions. Thus while the Japanese authorities were unable to come to terms with their predicament – because of objections by powerful but bankrupt businesses to foreclosure of their assets and political resistance to bailing out profligate banks[8] – the US taxpayer was readily co-opted (thanks to the powerful Wall Street lobby) to recapitalise the financial sector by

- bailing out insolvent Savings and Loan institutions (even though many of them were tainted by allegations of fraudulent bankruptcy – see Chapter 6) at an ultimate costs to the American taxpayer of $1.4 trillion; and

- manipulating the price of US treasury bills so as to hand huge capital gains to banks whose balance sheets had been devastated by imprudent lending.[9]

At the same time Scandinavian governments showed they were just as willing to spend taxpayers' money to bail out banks in a similar plight over real-estate losses – a disaster that can be clearly traced back to the results of financial liberalisation in the 1980s.[10] This fiasco resulted in the de facto nationalisation of most large banks in Finland, Norway and Sweden in the early 1990s.

What few observers were willing to recognise was the possibility that behind this difference in approach between Japan and other industrialised countries lay a common predicament in the shape of long-term stagnation in demand growth and shrinking outlets for investment. Hence although, by recapitalising their equally mismanaged financial sectors, the US and Scandinavian authorities were able in the short run to avoid the restraint to revived growth that continued to hang over their Japanese counterparts, they were in fact just postponing the day of reckoning. Indeed, as the events of the 1990s – culminating in the dotcom bubble in the closing years of the decade – were to reveal, the much hyped wonders of the 'new economy' were even more dependent on speculative fantasy than the Japanese bubble economy of the late 1980s.

Yet since the original problem stemmed from the same underlying cause – a compulsion to risky speculation induced by overcapacity and a consequent lack of genuinely remunerative investment opportunities in the real economy – it is arguable that the greater 'flexibility' of the US and Scandinavian authorities had merely served to delay the moment of truth. In fact, as was to become clear by the beginning of the new century, the Japanese collapse of 1990 should certainly have been seen as a portent of the inevitable fate of a hopelessly unbalanced global capitalist economy. Moreover, just as Japan has remained paralysed by its inability to remove market imbalances through necessary bankruptcies, so increasingly the United States and Europe have succumbed to the same tendency. For, in the wake of the millennium crash it was to become clear that these countries were, like Japan, weighed down with a growing number of 'zombie companies' (the living dead). The latter, which include such giants as United Airlines and the Fiat group of Italy, are protected from liquidation only by a combination of subsidy and the reluctance of both creditor banks and governments to face the financial and political costs of withdrawing their support.

Thus by the start of the 1990s there was plenty of evidence to show that both the Keynesian and neoclassical models had failed to cure the recurrent central weakness of capitalism and that a cyclical bust of colossal proportions was inevitable. Recognition of such reality could hardly have been further from public consciousness, however. For this conjuncture coincided with the final collapse of Soviet Communism, an event which Western propagandists readily proclaimed as the final victory of liberal capitalism not only over Communism but over any other imaginable economic system. Such uncritical rhetoric – most famously typified by the proclamation (which many affected to take seriously) of the 'end of history'[11] – helped to create a climate in which pressures for further liberalisation became irresistible. This was particularly true in relation to 'emerging markets' of the Third World and the former Soviet bloc, which in any case found they had no choice but to open up their markets to foreign capital and imports as a condition of receiving the aid they so desperately needed.

The unconscious irony of this triumphalism was to be harshly exposed as the 1990s unfolded. For the first half of the decade the

cheerleaders for the continuing trend to worldwide capitalist liberalisation – commonly referred to as globalisation – pointed to the
apparent huge success of certain emerging markets as a vindica-
tion of their ideology. It was even suggested that such supposedly
dynamic economies as those of East Asia – including not only the
original 'tigers' (South Korea, Taiwan, Hong Kong and Singapore)
but rapidly expanding Southeast Asian economies such as Thailand and Indonesia – might be harbingers of a 'Pacific century'
in which they would eclipse the allegedly declining economies of
the West. Yet almost before there was time to point out the numerous flaws in this scenario – the most obvious being that their apparent success was less attributable to applying Western precepts
of liberalisation than to traditional Eastern, state-orchestrated
dirigisme – it had been blown away by successive financial crises.
These began with that of Mexico (another vaunted neoliberal
emerging-market 'success story' on the Pacific Rim) in 1994–95
and culminated in the East Asian collapse of 1997–98.

Undaunted by such setbacks, neoliberal propagandists and their
supporting chorus of speculators and hype merchants were soon
able to whip up investor enthusiasm for a new prospective bonanza
– the high-tech boom driven particularly by telecommunications
and the Internet and centred on the United States. But as was soon
to be discovered, this supposed miracle was based on a manifestly
false prospectus (particularly in relation to the dotcom bubble of
1998–2000) and massive, reckless speculation. In truth it was not
hard to predict, as a number of commentators did at the height
of the 1990s boom,[12] that ultimate nemesis in the shape of a catastrophic financial collapse would be the inevitable outcome.

In fact, quite apart from the obviously manic and insubstantial
nature of this investment boom, it should have been clear from
the official statistics of GDP growth that projected returns based
on forecast earnings growth of 10 per cent a year were hopelessly

detached from reality. For these figures made it clear that average annual GDP growth in the industrialised countries as a whole would probably be lower in the 1990s than the previous decade – as indeed turned out to be the case (2.6 per cent compared with 2.8 per cent in the 1980s).[13] Moreover even the USA, which enjoyed a resurgence in growth during the late 1990s – at least on the basis of the probably inflated official statistics[14] – saw its overall average rate of GDP growth during the decade as a whole reach no more than 3 per cent a year, little more than that recorded in the 1980s and well below the 3.5 per cent achieved in the 1970s.[15]

By the time the crash began in March 2000 the markets had lost touch with economic reality to a quite unprecedented degree. The extent of the mania can perhaps best be illustrated by the fact that the market capitalisation (value) of the US stock market had by then risen to 181 per cent of national income (GDP) – compared with only 33 per cent at the start of the bull market in 1982. More tellingly still, this ratio was well over double that attained prior to the Wall Street crash of 1929 (81 per cent),[16] implying that the level of future corporate earnings growth being discounted by investors was far more wildly excessive than during the greatest market bubble of the twentieth century.

At the time of writing – over three years on from the start of the crash – the markets have already recorded the steepest fall from a previous peak since World War II (over 50 per cent in the case of the benchmark S&P 500 index in the USA). Moreover, given its still massive overvaluation compared with previous norms (see Chapter 2, Table 2.1), it is certain that it has much further to fall yet. Before assessing the full implications of this historic event for the future of the world economic order, however, it is appropriate to try and understand in more detail the forces that made possible the build-up to a financial crisis of such huge proportions.

2

The Deluge Postponed

We have observed how the post-World War II era of sustained high growth rates had by the 1970s induced an ingrained 'growth psychology' that effectively excluded any possibility of a significant or sustained downturn in business activity from the consciousness of entrepreneurs and policymakers alike. In other words, the global establishment had convinced itself that the traditional capitalist plague of the business cycle had been consigned to the history books. Moreover, the vast majority of both corporate and political leaders had become accustomed to the idea that business should properly depend on extensive support and protection from the state to sustain its level of activity. This was true whether or not they professed to believe in Keynesian principles of economic management – although perhaps few among them would sincerely have dissented from the conservative US president Richard Nixon when he declared in 1970 that 'we are all Keynesians now'.

Still more significantly, this expansionary mindset had made it possible, particularly in the United States, to build up large investment institutions – in the shape of mutual funds and pension funds – through which the savings of scores of millions of ordinary citizens were tied to the fortunes of the stock market. Hence when, in 1974, the markets plunged steeply for the first time since the war – by almost 50 per cent from its 1973 peak[1] – it was soon recognised that there was an acute danger of political as well as financial disaster.

Distorting market forces

A crucial action of the federal government designed to counteract this threat, as already noted, was to set up the Pensions Benefit Guaranty Corporation in 1974 to provide a safety net for pension funds. This mirrored the establishment of the Federal Deposit Insurance Corporation forty years earlier to provide statutory insurance of bank accounts following the mass bank failure of the early 1930s. The creation of such bodies gave clear expression to what was by then a vital, if ill-defined, commitment of governments throughout the industrialised world to act as 'lender of last resort' to the financial sector. This was true even though both these schemes were theoretically funded by insurance premiums from the beneficiary institutions. Thus it was not intended to be understood as an explicit guarantee of a state bail-out for any financial institution facing insolvency (since such a pledge would clearly undermine the essential principles of market capitalism based on risk and reward). Nevertheless, in practice it did mean that any bank deemed large enough for its insolvency to threaten the stability of the financial system as a whole was effectively assured of being bailed out by the state in that event.

The extension of such guarantees can be seen with hindsight as important milestones in the spread of 'moral hazard'. For inevitably banks now felt less and less constrained to apply strict prudential standards in determining whether borrowers were really creditworthy, confident in the belief that they would be bailed out with public money in the event of large-scale default. It was no coincidence that this process gathered momentum at a time when declining growth rates and stagnating demand were making it harder than ever for the corporate sector to satisfy the endless appetite of the market for more profits.

Clearly the central rationale for such distortions of the market – as for all other elements of economic policy – was and remains the overriding imperative of sustaining (and indeed maximising) the rate of economic growth. Indeed ever since World War II governments have proclaimed a high rate of growth to be the supreme public good, on the implied assumption that increasing the size of the cake would enable different claims on the national value-added (i.e. GDP) to be met more easily. What has perhaps been less generally recognised is that sustained high growth is above all vital to the health of the capitalist profits machine and to averting any lapse into cyclical decline. Yet it has undoubtedly been well understood by business leaders (even those not well versed in Marxian economics) that the ability of capitalist enterprises continually to reinvest their accumulated profits while sustaining the overall rate of profit depends crucially on continuous expansion of market demand.

This explains why the persistent theme of official policy has remained both (a) to focus on maximising growth as the key to raising living standards and (b) to insist that the key to achieving high growth is to give free rein to deregulated private enterprise. It also makes clear why this doctrine – the essence of the globalisation agenda and of the so-called Washington consensus – has been so dogmatically foisted on developing countries as a condition of their receiving aid.

From a capitalist perspective the theoretical logic of this policy stance is thus obvious. The equally obvious problem is that in practice it has proved impossible to deliver the hoped-for benefits. This reality is manifest, above all, in its failure not only to revive global growth rates but even to end the continuing steady decline that had begun in the 1970s – the extent of which (as noted in the last chapter) may even have been understated by the official statistics of GDP.

Yet for reasons already mentioned there has never been any question of acknowledgement by the political or business establishment that sustained growth at adequate levels might be unattainable, let alone that there might in consequence be a need for a radical modification of the 'free market' capitalist model. Rather there has been a resort to increasingly desperate expedients designed to (a) boost the growth of existing markets, (b) develop new markets as outlets for investment, and (c) maximise the rate of return from both new and existing investments. While in propaganda terms these have been presented as measures of liberalisation – and ending the 'dependency culture' – it has been hard to disguise the reality that the extensive role of the state in subsidising economic activity and enterprise has become an entrenched and indispensable prop to the system. The contradictory, and ultimately fatal, impact of this tendency – operating in a climate of reduced regulation and financial permissiveness – was to be increasingly exposed through the 1980s and 1990s.

Financial liberalisation

From around 1980 there were undertaken successive rounds of financial deregulation which, it was claimed by neoliberal ideologues, would 'unleash the forces of enterprise'. In the United States this meant removing most of the restraints to malpractice in the financial markets which had been introduced in the 1930s precisely in order to prevent a repetition of the fraud and excesses that had contributed so much to the market collapse of

1929–31. These 'reforms' – which were reflected in similar de-regulation initiatives elsewhere, particularly in other Anglo-Saxon countries – included

- progressively relaxing the de facto ban on quoted companies' buying back their own shares, which had been imposed in the 1930s in order to curb the ability of companies to manipulate their own share price;
- permitting banks, stockbrokers and other financial institutions to offer a full range of financial services within the same organisation – so that, for example, it could underwrite a public share offering by a company at the same time as advising investors on which securities to buy consistent with the optimal allocation of their funds. (In theory such obvious conflicts of interest were supposed to be avoided by establishing informal barriers – or 'Chinese walls' – separating them, but obviously without the possibility of any regulatory control.)[2]

It was not enough, however, to increase the flexibility of the corporate sector to take risks and manipulate the market price of securities. It was also implicitly understood that it would be necessary both to take steps to enhance the profitability of capital investment in general and also to find new outlets for investment, given the increasing saturation of consumer markets and intensifying competition. For only thus could it be ensured that investors would have the possibility of continuing to expand the flow of funds into new ventures and thereby maintain at least the semblance of a healthy profits system.

Sustaining the return on investment

Inevitably, a central plank of the neoliberal prospectus for reviving the economy has been the traditional capitalist response of trying to shift the burden of adjustment to the downward phase of the business cycle from the corporate sector to the rest of the economy. This naturally pointed to the necessity of (a) reducing the level of state intervention in and regulation of private enterprise (including the level of corporate taxation); and (b) squeezing wages and welfare benefits to employees and the unemployed alike. Hence the principal propaganda refrain of mainstream analysts by the 1980s was that the collapse of the post-war boom was to be laid at the door not of structural limits to growth but of excessive state intervention and of unaffordable wage and welfare levels in an increasingly competitive world. Yet, needless to say, there were no matching demands for restriction of the distorting measures of 'corporate welfare' – in the shape of state subsidies to private enterprise and investment – which had become so pervasive under the Keynesian model. On the contrary, there was a redoubled appetite for such benefits, on which private business had become just as dependent as the poor were by then on social welfare.[3]

In the continuing struggle to keep the capitalist growth model afloat it is important to understand the inescapable compulsion to fulfil two separate but related requirements:

- finding enough new outlets to absorb the ever expanding flow of investible funds inevitably generated by the profits system;[4]
- maintaining the rate of profit on old and new investments alike (or at least their market value).

In the late twentieth century the interrelationship between these two imperatives has exposed – perhaps as never before – the contradictory dynamics of what Karl Marx identified as 'capitalist accumulation'. For in so far as the search for profitable new investment outlets might have been successful in the short run, it only tended to compound the ongoing problem of maintaining the overall rate of profit, as it raised the cumulative stock of capital on which a return must be earned. Furthermore, the task of investors in trying to stay on this treadmill has been made all the harder to the extent that the rate of return demanded by the market has increased in response to competitive pressures. A crucial factor aggravating this tendency in recent decades has undoubtedly been the spread of pension funds and similar savings schemes (subsidised through tax breaks on contributions), which have channeled an ever growing flow of funds into securities markets. For this has had the effect of institutionalising the pressure for finding more investment outlets by creating a regular flow of new funds into the market regardless of the real demand for them at any particular time.

In fact the creation of this 'wall of money' may be seen as both exacerbating the problem and, paradoxically, providing relief from it (at least in the short run). This is because, while it obviously adds to the chronic oversupply of funds that has developed in the wake of stagnating market demand for investment capital, it also tends to force the institutions charged with deploying it to buy securities even when their price is high relative to the potential rate of return. In so far as the flow of funds can be maintained indefinitely — along with a plausible perception that the stocks concerned will continue to rise — it ensures that investment institutions will go on buying stocks and, in most cases, bid the price up still further. Hence while legions of investment analysts are employed to develop plausible stories as to why corporations can expect to improve the profitability of their operations — thus justifying a 'buy' recommendation for their shares — it has long been observed by the more serious financial journalists that the main factor sustaining prices is 'liquidity' (i.e. the wall of money).

Table 2.1 US stock market trends (Standard & Poor's 500, closing levels at 31 December)

	Index	Price/earnings ratio	Dividend yield (%)
1920	6.81	8.5	7.27
1930	15.34	15.8	5.62
1940	10.57	10.2	6.33
1950	20.41	7.2	7.20
1960	58.11	18.9	3.36
1970	92.15	17.3	3.41
1980	135.76	9.2	4.54
1990	330.22	15.2	3.66
1999	1469.25	33.3	1.14
2000	1320.28	24.6	1.19
2002	879.82	29.0	1.81
2003	1111.90	28.8	1.58

Source: Global Financial Data, www.globalfindata.com.

It is thus not surprising that there has been a progressive rise in the proportion of total returns from equity investments that is accounted for by capital appreciation rather than actual earnings (profits), whether retained or distributed. While it is difficult to quantify this trend with any precision,[5] it can clearly be inferred from the stock market trends illustrated in Table 2.1 that during the long bull market of 1982–2000 capital appreciation came to represent the lion's share of total returns. This is particularly apparent from the fact that by the end of 1999 (virtually the peak of the market) the average price-to-earnings ratio had risen to 33.3 – close to double the peak levels achieved either before the Great Crash of 1929 or during the previous stock market boom of the 1960s and early 70s. These unprecedentedly stretched valuations are also mirrored in dividend yields that fell to little over

1 per cent by the late 1990s – well under half the lowest level ever previously recorded.[6]

The only conceivable justification for such high prices – and one often used by market analysts – was that they might be seen as discounting high levels of future earnings growth. Yet against a background of continuing relative stagnation in the world economy, punctuated by increasingly frequent financial crises throughout the 1980s and 1990s, it may seem incredible that investors could have been taken in by projections that corporate earnings would rise by 10 per cent or more a year indefinitely.[7] In reality, it can be safely assumed that they were scarcely concerned by earnings prospects at all, and that they were simply betting that prices would be swept ever higher by the dynamics of the wall of money. It is thus clear that the flow of investment funds into the securities markets has since the early 1980s been increasingly driven by speculative forces rather than any consideration of the real economic value of the underlying assets. Yet it should also be obvious that this extremely dangerous tendency – greatly facilitated by a combination of financial deregulation and official incentives to invest – was the unavoidable consequence of the expansion of institutional investment funds. For these were effectively compelled to pour large sums of money in fixed annual contributions into one kind of security or another regardless of their objective value (in terms of actual or potential earnings).

Indeed nothing illustrates better the pernicious impact of combining quasi-Keynesian state support for the private sector with liberalisation (backed up by a sustained media campaign of uncritical propaganda and pro-market hype) in creating the conditions for an unavoidable financial crisis – which is thus bound to be on a scale far greater than any previous one.

Few will find it surprising perhaps that governments and media alike have sought to ignore or conceal this reality of stagnating growth and overvalued shares, trying instead to emphasise the positive at all times and present this era of liberalisation as the triumphant rebirth of capitalism. Inevitably, however, this sustained act of mass deception (in which the establishment has seemingly come to believe in its own propaganda) has had disastrous consequences, in that

- not only has it precluded any attempt to address the fundamental weakness of a global economic system whose satisfactory functioning depends on sustaining high rates of growth which in reality are unattainable, but
- it has also encouraged widespread fraud and corruption on the part of leaders of the financial and corporate sectors. For it was hardly to be expected that such powerful figures – encouraged to treat their corporate and personal interests as identical with the public interest and at the same time to see profit maximisation as the supreme virtue – would not succumb to the lure of moral hazard.

This evident determination on the part of government and corporate leaders to mislead the public was mirrored within large parts of the economics profession. This was demonstrated, in particular, by the increasingly perverse emphasis in economic management on the 'supply side' – that is, the belief that the way to maximise economic growth was to remove regulations or fiscal disincentives to the expansion of investment and production. As well as obviously pointing to a need for greater deregulation and liberalisation, this perspective also naturally emphasised lower taxes on business (and implicitly also greater subsidies).

What such prescriptions blatantly ignored was the possibility that inadequate demand could be a limiting factor, as most economists in the 1960s (when Keynesian ideas predominated) would have quickly, and correctly, pointed out. Thus in the United States

from the 1980s – and even more so in the 1990s – the success of
the economy in maintaining supposedly 'strong' growth, and its
capacity to continue doing so, were claimed by leading officials
and economists to depend on its rising productivity based on
investment in new technology. Even after the bubble had burst in
2000 none other than the chairman of the Federal Reserve Board,
Alan Greenspan, and the chairman of President Bush's Council
of Economic Advisers, Glenn Hubbard, persistently claimed that
rising productivity would boost the economy by strengthening
demand. In reality, as elementary economic theory demonstrates,
it would obviously have had the opposite effect – to the extent
that the reduced need for labour per unit of output would naturally tend to reduce aggregate employment and personal incomes.
Likewise policymakers' obsession with the supply side rather than
the demand side has seemingly blurred their perception of the
familiar truth that, while consumption may be stimulated beyond
the level of disposable income by reducing the cost of credit, this
can only be done by 'borrowing consumption from the future'. In
other words it is bound to be at the expense of long-run demand
and output growth once the credit has to be repaid. Hence governments' increasing tendency to use what has become their only
instrument of demand management, changes in interest rates, to
induce consumers to take on more and more debt in a desperate
effort to boost economic activity, apparently heedless of the fact
that such an artificial boost to demand is bound to be matched
by a subsequent downturn.

Rise of the bubble economy

For a short while in the 1980s it might have been forgivable that
serious analysts should have suspended disbelief in this neoliberal
prospectus. Following the renewed recession at the start of the

decade global growth rebounded from 1984 to 1989 – though still nowhere near to the levels of the 1960s – while at the same time the euphoria generated by financial liberalisation and the investment opportunities presented by new technology fuelled a stock market boom. Yet once this financial boom had been brought to earth by the market 'crash' of 1987 and the subsequent inflationary bubble (notably in real estate) had collapsed in scandal and renewed economic slowdown in 1990–92,[8] there should have been no further room for doubt as to the inevitable failure of the neoliberal experiment.

However, as already noted, there was a single-minded determination on the part of the ruling elite not to confront such reality. Rather, the response to renewed financial failure at the start of the 1990s was a concerted effort by the authorities in the industrialised countries to rescue failing institutions from their folly and restore confidence in the markets as quickly as possible. In the USA this was notably demonstrated in the bail-out of the Savings and Loan institutions – many of them reduced to insolvency by management abuses amounting to fraud following their deregulation in the early 1980s – at a cost to the taxpayer of as much as $1.4 trillion. Inevitably, however, this state-sponsored recapitalisation of the financial sector simply paved the way for even more speculative excess. For in the absence of a really severe downturn – permitting a genuine shakeout of excess capacity in line with the normal course of the business cycle – the only result was bound to be a further round of overinvestment or speculative bidding up of asset values to inflated levels. In fact the most conspicuous features of the 1990s economy proved to be

- an even greater surge of investment flows into the emerging markets – provoking a succession of crises, starting with the Mexican meltdown of 1994 and culminating in the East

Asian crash of 1997–98, which marked the final bursting of that bubble; and

- a manic boom in a number of largely insubstantial investment fads on the basis of heavily hyped new technology, notably in the field of telecommunications and the related growth of the Internet (see Chapter 3).

Technology: the new enemy

Compounding the traditional constraint of consumer market saturation in recent decades has been the impact of rapid technological change – a quite novel feature of latter-day capitalism in relation to previous business cycles. This phenomenon, whose significance has been largely ignored or dismissed by mainstream analysts, is reflected in a transformation in the scale and nature of the demand for investment capital. It has arisen mainly because improved technology (particularly the increased computerisation of most mechanical processes) has made it possible to improve the productivity of capital – facilitating a much higher volume and value of output for each pound or dollar invested. Such tendencies may largely help to explain the fact that, over most of the 1970–2000 period, the growth rate of fixed capital formation in OECD countries slowed down even more than that of aggregate GDP. Moreover, it is notable that much of the fixed investment that did take place (particularly in the 1980s) was in cost-cutting techniques that permitted substantial returns on investment even against a background of minimal market growth – a possibility previously discounted by most economists.[9]

A related and highly significant development stemming from advances in information technology in particular has been a change in the very nature of the capital assets of enterprise. This has entailed a shift from the traditional importance of fixed assets towards increasing emphasis on the intangible ones of human capital needed for the new more 'knowledge-intensive' industries that have emerged. An associated phenomenon has been the rise in importance of service industries in the overall economy, reflecting the changing pattern of demand, particularly in the industrialised countries, as consumption of most goods (including durables as well as food and clothing) has reached saturation. Such industries also tend to be less capital-intensive than traditional manufacturing, while those in the field of entertainment (notably pop music, sport or cinema) may for obvious reasons be described as 'talent-intensive' – that is, heavily dependent on high-cost human capital.[10] The overall long-term impact of such trends is dramatically reflected in a reported decline in the proportion of the total value (debt and equity) of US quoted non-financial companies that is accounted for by the book value of their tangible assets from 83 per cent in 1978 to 31 per cent in 1998.[11]

This has obviously given an added twist to the decline in demand for investment capital, since human capital assets (in the shape of highly skilled or talented individuals with potentially very valuable expertise) are by definition not fixed and cannot therefore be outlets for capital investment as conventionally understood. By the same token, such 'assets' can only be valued on a balance sheet (if at all) with extreme uncertainty, as their potential for generating income streams depends not only on their remaining in the company but on whether their particular talents retain value in a world of fluid markets and rapidly changing technology.[12] One response to this trend may be seen in the growing concern of major corporations to try and establish their 'intellectual property' rights in new technological advances – for example, by patenting genetically modified crop varieties and even the human genome.

The significance of this little-noticed change in the relationship between technology and capital can hardly be overstated. For it means we are now confronted with a situation where not only is there a classic crisis of overinvestment and overcapacity typical of the capitalist business cycle, but technological change is rendering profit-maximising capital increasingly redundant and/or ill-suited to meeting the needs of the evolving pattern of economic enterprise. These two tendencies (one old and one new) would seem bound to threaten the continued acceptability of the capitalist profits system as the basis for economic society in the twenty-first century. This is all the more true in a world where the willingness of the enfranchised masses – increasingly attuned to the idea that minimum standards of living and individual economic dignity are basic human rights – to make sacrifices to a fickle capitalist god is more doubtful than ever.

To what extent the global capitalist establishment and the investor community have grasped the reality of such threats to the system to which they have dedicated their lives and on the survival of which their continued wealth and power depends is hard to determine. Ironically, it is the Internet – briefly perceived at the turn of the century to be the vehicle for a capitalist re-birth – which has come to be recognised by some as perhaps the most potent threat to the system's well-being. Thus at the very height of the mania in 1999 the leading American investor Warren Buffett noted that it was 'a big positive for consumers but a big negative for investors'. The perceptiveness of this observation has been confirmed more recently by the chief executive of the Japanese consumer electronics giant Sony, Noboyuki Idei, who has pointed out the threat posed to his company's traditional business model by the free, direct access to information and entertainment provided by the Internet.[13] Such thoughts might well be echoed by all the leading players in the video and recorded music industries, not to mention telecommunications operators, who will soon find that all broadband users will be able to make telephone calls free of time charges.

Despite this evidence that new technology can be at least as much a threat to, as an opportunity in relation to, the goal of perpetuating a dynamic capitalism, there are few outward signs of doubt disturbing the unanimous and euphoric belief in the 'free market' and globalisation expressed by the mass media and mainstream political parties. On the other hand, many features of the neoliberal capitalist economy as it has evolved since around 1980 betray an underlying malaise among corporate leaders and the politicians so easily co-opted to do their bidding.

The search for new investment outlets

In the face of such threats, both traditional and new, to the stability of the global capitalist economy – particularly at the 'mature' stage of the business cycle – it is not surprising to find there has been an intensive effort to find new outlets for investment capital. Naturally, this compulsion has gone hand in hand with continuing pressure to exploit every available opportunity to extract more value from existing businesses in the face of increasingly stagnant demand and the consequent decline in capacity utilisation and intensification of competition. Among other expressions of this syndrome has been the further expansion of the boundaries of decency and taste in the direction already indicated by the breakdown in the 1970s of taboos such as those on gambling and pornography (see Chapter 1). Indeed at the time of writing the New Labour government in Britain is preparing a further 'modernisation' of the gambling laws which would potentially turn every town in the country into a mini Las Vegas. Another recent notable symptom of this tendency has been the resort by the increasingly moribund advertising industry to targeting children openly – even though this has traditionally been regarded as unacceptable on the rather obvious grounds that it amounts to exploitation of the immature and financially irresponsible.[14] This development may also be plausibly linked to the growing trend of treating children as young adults for commercial purposes and the apparently related mushrooming of child pornography and paedophile crime.[15]

Quite how far such anti-social developments may be laid at the door of owners of capital seeking to resist its increasing redundancy – and consequent devaluation – may be open to dispute. What is far less disputable is that such resistance to both cyclical and long-term trends in the market have given rise to a search for new investment outlets that has become progressively more irrational and surreal – as described in the next chapter.

3

The Surfeit of Capital and Its Consequences

The growing frustration of private enterprise from the 1970s at the difficulty in finding profitable outlets to which capital could be recycled has been reflected in the targeting of some surprising new areas of economic activity. Thus the 1980s saw the emergence of a number of investment fads covering broad fields which previously had been either ignored or else considered of little importance.

The plundering of the public sector

While private commercial interests had always more or less covertly used the resources of the state to bolster their profitability, the post-war era of Keynesian, 'mixed economy' capitalism had effectively sanctified the public subsidy of the private sector as a normal and essential feature of a modern economy. It was thus in a sense quite natural that those committed to perpetuating an economic system dominated by the private sector at the end of the twentieth century should have sought to utilise all the assets and powers of the state to this end.

Privatisation

From the early days of industrial capitalism in the nineteenth century it had been widely accepted that vital public services and utilities – such as water and energy supply, telecommunications and public education – should be largely provided by organisations owned and controlled by the state (whether at national or local level). This view was based on the perception that such services were either (a) 'natural monopolies' – that is, because of the infrastructure needed to deliver them it was not feasible to subject them to any meaningful form of competition; (b) so essential (requiring uninterrupted provision) that any possibility that the suppliers might be forced by financial pressures to curtail service was unacceptable; or (c) so inherently unprofitable (as in the case of public education) that private capital could not be expected to regard it as an attractive opportunity.

Over time indeed there was a tendency for other services (and even manufacturing enterprises) to be taken over or created by the state where their diminished profitability reduced the commitment of private owners to provide the kind of service or product required by the public (as with the railways in Britain during World War I and collapsed banks in continental Europe and elsewhere in the 1930s), or where the private sector was seen as unwilling or unable to support needed investment in the automotive or chemical industries (as in pre-war Germany and Italy). Even in the United States, where there was a strong ideological aversion to public ownership, state regulation combined with subsidy (as well as selective public investment) was accepted in many sectors, particularly after the disastrous financial collapse of 1929–31. Thus, for example, the telecommunications industry was for decades a highly regulated monopoly until the Clinton administration tried to open it up to competition in the 1990s.

Notwithstanding these historical realities, it rapidly became the conventional wisdom in the 1980s (following the lead of the Thatcher government in Britain) that the public sector had failed adequately to provide the services that had hitherto been largely seen as its preserve, and that the private sector – driven by its supposed inherent capacity to achieve greater cost-effectiveness than the state sector – should take them over. Surprisingly, none of the proponents of this argument ever felt it necessary to explain why, if it were valid, it had ever been decided to establish these services in the public sector in the first place. A slightly more plausible reason for privatising them was the fact that growing public-sector deficits had reduced the state's capacity to provide the necessary investment – although it should have been obvious that this was largely a self-fulfilling prophecy (see below).

What was never stated by the advocates of such privatisation was that it also offered a much needed outlet for surplus investment funds generated by the private sector. Had this been understood, the grotesquely absurd irony of the whole privatisation trend would have been revealed. For in essence what happened was that

- state revenues were reduced through tax cutting – of which a major purpose was to boost the rate of corporate profits;
- the state was thereby prevented from making adequate investment in public utilities and services;
- the resulting gap could only be filled by the investment of the additional private profits (for which there were few, if any, other outlets), which would not have existed – and would not have been needed – but for the tax cuts.

Another fundamental flaw in the whole ideology of privatisation was exposed when, in response to growing pressure from neoliberal extremists and (mainly US) commercial interests, it was applied to inherently non-commercial public services such as education and prisons. For this entailed the creation of a wholly artificial market for these services – so that private profits must ultimately be underwritten by the state as sole provider of funds – casting obvious doubt on the claim that such an arrangement could possibly be in the interests of either users or taxpayers.

Public sector debt

Just as the squeeze on public finances (partly induced by tax cuts) served to bolster the case for privatisation, so it also helped to generate another outlet for the private sector's surplus of investment capital. For while the most vocal enthusiasts for tax cutting – the so-called supply-side school of economists that flourished briefly in the early 1980s – claimed that it would actually result in an improvement in the fiscal balance by stimulating higher growth and thus higher aggregate tax revenues, few were probably surprised that deficits continued to rise (see Chapter 1).

Although this trend has rightly been viewed as a cause for concern, there is no doubt that it has also been seen by the financial establishment as an investment opportunity, involving as it does the issue of hundreds of billions of dollars' worth of 'gilt-edged' government bonds every year. The fact that the issue of so much public debt has created a severe debt-service burden for the future may be a secondary consideration for an investor community preoccupied with maximising the short-term return on its capital. On the other hand the efforts to curb public borrowing from the late 1990s – particularly in the newly constituted euro currency zone[1] – evidently reflect official recognition of the unsustainability of continuous deficit financing from the perspective of maintaining both budgetary and currency stability. Yet the resulting slight reversal of the rise in public debt in OECD countries – down to around 74 per cent of GDP by 2000–01 – has been deplored by some in the financial community, particularly as pension funds have come to feel the need for more secure bond investments in the face of collapsing equity markets. In Britain there have even been calls for the government to follow the example of Australia and engage in 'overfunding' – that is, borrowing more than it needs – in order to provide pension funds with enough safe assets to invest in.[2] Yet the British government may have felt it had already done quite enough to subsidise the fund managers by issuing long-dated stock at interest rates well above those prevailing in the market.[3]

Although by the late 1990s investors may have come to feel there was insufficient further scope for exploiting the public debt market in the industrialised countries, they were increasingly willing to seek out, or indeed to try and create, similar opportunities in Third World or 'emerging' markets. For fund managers this approach also fitted with their need to meet increasingly demanding target levels of return by deliberately targeting high-risk bonds, given that they offered higher rates of interest. Moreover, to the extent that they could co-opt the International Monetary Fund (IMF) and Western governments to distort the market in their favour – by getting them to support high fixed exchange rates in the issuing countries – they were able to obtain superprofits from these assets, at least for a while (see Chapter 4). Thus the whole financial establishment has been able to extend to a global scale its de facto conspiracy to undermine public finances by treating the state as 'borrower of last resort'.[4]

The appetite for high risk

This pressure to seek out high-risk assets as the returns from
more conventional investments proved increasingly inadequate in
a profit-squeezed world was expressed in the enthusiasm for other
new investment fashions in the 1980s and 1990s.

'Emerging' markets

An outlet which suddenly became the object of unprecedented attention from investors in the industrialised countries from around
1980 was that provided by developing (or Third World) countries.
This new vogue might have been thought an even more surprising change of heart than the enthusiasm for privatisation which
started about the same time. This is because over the preceding
thirty years, in which most of these countries had achieved their
formal independence from colonial rule, they had come to be
viewed as largely no-go areas for Western investors, except to the
extent that they possessed significant petroleum or other scarce
mineral resources. The obvious reasons for their basic unattrac-
tiveness to foreign capital were their typical deficiencies in terms
of having small markets, unstable governments, weak currencies
and at best unpredictable policies with regard to the freedom to
transfer funds abroad.[5]

Objectively, it is hard to see what change had occurred in the
situation of most developing countries by the 1980s which could
have justified the new-found enthusiasm of foreign companies
and financial institutions for investing in what they began to refer
to as emerging markets. For this term, clearly implying that the
economies concerned were on the brink of some kind of 'take-
off' to a more mature level of development and stability, would
have been hard to justify in respect of the vast majority, whose
prospects had in fact clearly deteriorated in line with the world

economy during the 1970s, with many having suffered particularly badly from the successive oil 'shocks'. Virtually the only exceptions to this rule were a small number of countries in East Asia (notably South Korea, Taiwan, Singapore and Hong Kong) which had been enabled to achieve high levels of growth based mainly on the development of effectively subsidised exports of manufactured goods. Such developments received a further boost as intensifying competitive pressures in the industrial market economies induced Japanese and other companies to locate more capacity in developing countries so as to take advantage of lower labour costs. Yet although this process was facilitated by moves to make such economies more friendly to foreign capital (notably by relaxing foreign exchange controls), it was difficult for anyone familiar with the Third World at the time to see why this should have been the basis of a sustained investment bonanza. In the event such scepticism was to prove all too well founded (see Chapter 4).

Corporate mergers and acquisitions

The takeover of one company by another had long been a defining feature of the capitalist market place. Indeed for many champions of the system it was one of its most admirable manifestations, in that it was a vivid demonstration of the supposed dynamic of efficient resource allocation made possible by the free operation of market forces – as weaker enterprises were absorbed by stronger ones. Yet it had to be conceded that its benefits in terms of economic efficiency were only attainable to the extent that anti-monopoly regulation was effective – a realisation which posed the most serious limitation on mergers in mature capitalist economies. For it was generally held that any company acquiring more than about a third of any national market for a given product would have too much market power for this to be consistent with genuine competition. Increasingly, therefore, from the 1960s profitable companies in search of investment outlets for the reinvestment of their surplus profits had felt compelled to diversify into sectors often far removed from their 'core' activities (e.g. combining telephone equipment manufacture with hotel chains in the same group of companies).

This process of creating 'conglomerates' continued through subsequent decades, even though the capacity of such mergers to yield benefits for shareholders was viewed with scepticism by those who wondered whether the business skills that had brought success in one sector could necessarily be applied as effectively in another. Remarkably, however, such doubts were later used to turn the logic of the takeover process on its head, as many conglomerates were themselves acquired by groups with the aim of breaking them up into more specialist units which were then presented as better able to enhance shareholder value. The willingness of the investor community to swallow such seemingly contradictory reasoning was no doubt greatly assisted by the cult of the manager and the dealmaker – a phenomenon of the 1980s and 1990s which induced many to believe in the almost magical powers of certain individuals to identify and realise hidden value in previously unconsidered assets. This irrational faith was barely shaken by the financial crisis of 1990–91, which exposed the hollowness of most of the hype and revealed many of the heroes of the 1980s' financial boom as criminals – in the wake of the collapse of the market for 'junk' bonds and the exposure of other shady methods used to manipulate asset prices.

In the light of such setbacks and the continuing evidence that corporate mergers generally have added little value from the perspective of either shareholders or the wider economy,[6] it is remarkable that the global flow of funds into mergers and acquisitions continued to rise through the 1990s – from US$349 billion in 1988 to a peak of over $3 trillion in 2000.[7] In fact there are strong grounds for concluding that the trend was mainly driven by a combination of

- The difficulty experienced by corporate managers in extracting adequate profits from organic growth of their existing businesses (for the reasons given in Chapter 2) and a consequent tendency to see takeovers of other companies as a way of adding to shareholder value without having to take uncomfortable decisions. In other words, as succinctly put by an eminent management guru, from the perspective of corporate management 'dealmaking beats working'.[8] In similar vein it has been said of General Electric – as of 2000 the most valuable and publicly admired corporation in the USA – that it 'is increasingly like a large shark: it must keep moving, and keep eating, or perish'.[9] Equally, in the still more competitive climate to which some sectors (such as telecommunications) are exposed in the post-crash era, mergers with apparently more profitable businesses are seen by financially squeezed companies (and their bankers) as a means of escaping their doom – at least in the short run.[10]
- The powerful incentive for investment banks to obtain a bigger share of the extremely lucrative business of mergers and acquisitions, where their advisory role can bring them commissions and fees running to tens of millions of dollars for each deal. This has been reflected in high-pressure marketing strategies targeting the chief executives and directors of those major corporations which they perceive to be potentially receptive to the idea of pursuing a takeover. It is noteworthy, moreover, that the powers of persuasion of the newly emerged financial conglomerates formed as a result of financial liberalisation

(including Citigroup, Merrill Lynch and Goldman Sachs) have also included personal offers to directors of client corporations to take up highly profitable share issues in unrelated companies[11] (see also Chapter 4).

This combination of incompetence and corruption among top executives ensured that misguided mergers would play a big part in many of the major corporate collapses (notably that of the telecommunications giant WorldCom) that were to follow the bursting of the stock market bubble in 2000. Even among companies that did not collapse, moreover, it was found that many if not most such deals destroyed value rather than increasing it, as the vaunted 'synergies' of mergers failed to materialise. The most notorious example of this during the period was the $106 billion merger of the US Internet service provider AOL with the media giant Time Warner in 1999, which after the crash required a massive balance sheet write-down leading to the biggest quarterly corporate loss in US history ($54 billion).

As was to become clear in the successive financial crises that unfolded from the mid-1990s, such investment fads as those described above were driven more by speculation than by any genuine belief that they could result in a sustained improvement in the earnings yield of the company shares affected. In other words, the perception of most professional investors, including the pension funds and other institutions which increasingly dominated the market, was that the profit from such investments was to come from buying stocks cheap and selling them dear rather than holding them for any long-term income stream they might produce (a conclusion supported by the stock market price trends of the 1990s – see Chapter 2). Such a tendency was greatly encouraged and facilitated by the liberalisation of financial markets. For this made it much easier both to manipulate the price of shares and to promote their sale at ever higher prices to the unsuspecting public, particularly as the latter were constantly being urged by their governments to buy into the allegedly huge benefits of the 'shareholder democracy'.

Just as important as deregulation in facilitating this shift to speculation – or in investor parlance from 'value' to 'growth' stocks – was the climate of enthusiastic belief in the wealth-creating potential of the 'liberated' capitalist marketplace which was nurtured by the whole establishment, particularly in the Anglo-Saxon countries. The media in particular generated enormous hype surrounding leading entrepreneurs and the great wealth they were supposedly creating for themselves and many others. In Britain the Thatcher administration sought to underpin this admiration for the new 'masters of the universe'[12] by (among other things) handing out free or discounted shares in privatised utilities to millions of ordinary people for whom the world of finance and investment was largely alien. For while at one level this can be seen as simply a vote-buying ploy at the taxpayers' expense, it was also evidently intended to convince the masses that they too could be a part of the new magical get-rich-quick world.

High-tech fantasies

As the world's major governments responded to the financial crises of the 1990s with further bouts of credit expansion and recapitalisation of insolvent institutions – still setting their faces against any major destruction of capital – they ensured, perhaps unwittingly, that investors would pursue new investment outlets with greater recklessness than ever. This was most conspicuously demonstrated by the so-called 'dotcom bubble' of the late 1990s, the bursting of which in March 2000 finally precipitated the stock market collapse that was still blighting the global economy in 2004.

This coincidence of the advent of the Internet and the availability of a virtually unlimited supply of investment funds thanks to the extreme permissiveness of the monetary authorities, particularly in the United States, led to the promotion of thousands of commercial ventures trading in cyberspace. The implicit presumption employed to sell this concept to investors was that the new sales medium could generate huge extra demand for established consumer products and services based on the low selling costs (and hence reduced prices) achievable through the new medium. In reality the whole business model was in almost every case inherently implausible given that (a) there was no empirical evidence that consumers would switch to Internet buying in large numbers; nor that (b) if they did so profits would be more than marginally interesting, given the relative ease with which competitors could imitate it. Yet such glaring weaknesses did not prevent hundreds of billions of dollars being subscribed for such ventures. The predictable result, as all the dotcom startups burnt through vast quantities of cash without generating any profits (and in some cases barely any sales), was an investment debacle on a scale to match that of historic manias such as the eighteenth-century South Sea Bubble.

However, the folly of the dotcom bubble was far from being an isolated aberration. Of the many other examples of perverse misallocation of resources that have occurred since the start of the 1990s a few notable ones serve to demonstrate the dire consequences of the all-pervading pressure on investor institutions to identify remotely plausible opportunities for investing large sums of the investing public's money.

Telecommunications

This was an industry where technological innovation actually attracted a far greater inflow of investment funds (no less than $4 trillion worldwide) than did the dotcom industry itself – a sector with which the telecommunications boom was seen by investors as being closely linked. It was probably also inspired to some extent by the undoubted success of mobile telephony based on cellular technology. This phenomenon, arguably the sole mass-market consumer product success of the 1990s, combined with moves to deregulate and privatise telecommunications utilities all over the world (most notably the US Telecommunications Act of 1996) to induce a surge of investor 'bullishness' over prospects for the sector as a whole. This was further underpinned by official hype over the projected growth of the 'information superhighway', suggesting that there could be a bonanza in the demand for telecommunications services. The result was a misallocation of investment funds with few, if any, parallels in history. Two particular examples of the waste involved are worthy of mention:

- *Fibre-optic cable*   This glass-based product, long recognised as vastly more cost-effective than traditional copper cables for carrying telecommunications traffic, suddenly began to attract huge volumes of investment in the 1990s on the assumption of massive traffic growth to come. This was seen as being particularly linked to the growth of demand for 'bandwidth' as a function of the expected Internet boom. Yet quite apart from the obvious uncertainty over the latter, optimism has in any case been tempered by the fact that even by the mid-1990s mobile (wireless) networks were already starting to take an increasing share of voice traffic. In the event by the middle of 2001 some 20 million miles of fibre-optic cable had been installed worldwide, of which only 5 per cent was in use, suggesting there was enough capacity to meet demand growth for many decades if not centuries to come. The most notable corporate casualty of this profligacy was Global Crossing Inc. – subject of one of the largest bankruptcy filings in US history in 2002, with estimated losses of at least $20 billion.

- *Satellite mobile telephones* In the late 1990s no fewer than three international consortia were formed to invest in satellite-based mobile telephone systems on the basis that this would meet a demand for handsets that could be used anywhere in the world, including places that were out of reach of cellular systems. However, this concept, which led to the investment of more than $6 billion in launching three competing satellite networks, ignored the fact that cellular network coverage (much cheaper to use) was approaching 95 per cent of the world's populated areas and that fixed satellite terminals were already available for those locations (e.g. sea-going vessels) that needed them. Most incredibly of all, no mention was made, in the publicity, of the fact that the devices would not function in enclosed spaces such as buildings.

For shareholders the consequence of this collective foolishness was a loss on their investments in the telecommunications industry worldwide amounting to a staggering $2.5 trillion – equal to one-quarter of US GDP – between March 2000 (the start of the crash) and the middle of 2002. With hindsight they might have wondered how they (or rather their fund managers and investment advisors) could have become so disconnected from reality as to ignore the fact that average household spending on telecommunications in the USA had stabilised at around $1,000 a year – and hence could not reasonably be considered to have much growth potential.

Biotechnology: illusion and reality

Another sector where technological advance has excited investors since the 1980s has been that of biotechnology, based largely on exploiting the supposed potential of developments in genetic research, particularly in relation to the pharmaceuticals industry. Yet although the unsatisfied demand for new treatments for numerous diseases (notably cancer) is huge and potentially very lucrative, it has proved hard to turn the promise of this sector into reality. The huge cost of research and development – whose results are all too often abortive – has meant that initial investor enthusiasm for new ventures in this field has very often turned to disappointment. In fact it has long been understood that success for new enterprises in this field requires a combination of public subsidy and risk funding from venture-capital institutions during a start-up phase that must be expected to last several years. The growing recognition of such harsh realities led to demands in Britain in 2003 for even higher tax breaks and support from public funds – to match those received by the US industry, where stock market valuations of the sector have held up better.[13]

Genetically modified crops: perverting the course of the market

Aside from the irrational folly of promoting investment in products in the telecoms sector for which there was a priori little or no demand, the biotechnology industry provides what is perhaps a unique case study of trying to fabricate demand for products. This concerns the hotly disputed attempt to promote genetically modified (GM) varieties of crops developed by leading multinational suppliers of planting material and agro-chemicals. While it may be far from definitively proved whether or not such GM crops can be considered safe from the point of view of human health or the environment, there is unquestionably extensive resistance to their introduction outside the United States – where most of the companies supplying them are based. This resistance is based on a number of factors, including

- Widespread suspicion (particularly in Europe) of the potential dangers of new 'high-tech' food products in the wake of the damage resulting from BSE ('mad cow disease') and its human equivalent in the 1980s and 1990s; and
- The lack of any compelling evidence that there is a need for new varieties with the potential to boost crop yields in a world where the technical capacity for food production already far exceeds potential consumption. (Predictably, supporters of GM crops have pointed to the existence of famine and malnutrition in certain parts of the world as evidence of the need for them, ignoring the well-established truth that these scourges are generally the result of poverty and problems other than inadequate crop varieties.)

Because of the substantial investment by US corporations in the development of GM crops, the refusal of the EU and other countries to license their use has been made into a major trade dispute between the USA and the EU, with the former accusing the latter of covert protectionism. But what is most remarkable about this dispute is the determination of the USA to try to compel other countries not only to license products which public opinion clearly distrusts but to try to deprive people of the right to choose between food products based on GM and non-GM varieties. Thus attempts by the EU to insist that, if and when GM products are licensed, the distinction be made clear through labelling have resulted in the US government threatening to object to this also as unjustified protectionism. In short, the USA is apparently insisting that Europeans and others should be forced to eat GM-based food whether they like it or not. It seems hard to believe that such an attempt at perversion of the notion of consumer sovereignty (supposedly an article of faith among those who are fond of proclaiming the essential link between the market economy and 'freedom') will be allowed to succeed. If it were to happen it would surely be a sign that capitalism had, ironically, sunk to the level of the failed totalitarian Soviet economy – by forcing consumers to consume what the authorities choose to supply rather than what they want.

Energy trading: the industry nobody needed

Perhaps an even more extraordinary case of a product or service developed to serve the interests of corporate investors rather than – or even at the expense of – consumers has been that of energy trading. This activity, which was the principal line of business of the Enron Corporation at the time of its spectacular bankruptcy in 2001, was developed in order to meet the supposed demand for intermediaries between the primary suppliers of energy (oil, gas or electricity) and those distributing the end product. In fact this type of business only grew up after the deregulation of the power industry in the USA and elsewhere from the late 1980s seemed to offer opportunities for more competitive trading of energy. Until the collapse of Enron virtually nobody had noticed that in fact this was an inherently flawed business model in that it did not actually involve adding any real value to the product. In the words of one expert, 'in essence, traders would buy a finished good, flip it a number of times – adding no economic value – and call it a business'.[14]

Consequently, once Enron and its competitors had ceased trading in this field, utilities were able to resume direct trading between themselves without any adverse effect on their operations:

It is as if the energy trading market has disappeared in a puff of smoke, and nobody knows it has gone. Nobody, that is, but [the traders'] former employees and the shareholders and lenders who staked billions of dollars on the prospects of energy traders [but who are] now rushing for the exits.[15]

Among those who had been seduced into believing in this particular set of emperor's clothes, it may be noted, were some of the most revered global corporations, who might perhaps have been expected to know better. Thus Royal Dutch Shell, seeing how much money Enron appeared to be making from energy trading in the late 1990s, called in McKinsey, the world's most respected consultancy group, to help devise a scheme for selling gas to power-generating utilities on a long-term basis in return for an option to sell the power generated. In order to make the deal appear profitable, however, it was necessary to assume unrealistically high price projections for power. By 2002, however, it was already clear that the overoptimism built into this plan could mean the total amount invested in it by Shell ($7.4 billion) would have to be written off.[16]

The fact that such a variety of actors from business, government and the mass media colluded to promote so much investment in so many concepts of inherently doubtful, or obviously non-existent, value is in itself a damning comment on the state of latter-day world capitalism. Yet given the unbreakable commitment of the ruling establishment to resist – by all possible means – the inexorable re-emergence of the business cycle, such seemingly irrational conduct appears all too logical. Predictably, however, propaganda, subsidy and market distortion would ultimately prove insufficient to keep the ship afloat.

4

The Dishonesty of Desperation

It has been observed that pressures on the corporate sector to maintain the growth of shareholder value intensified throughout the 1980s and 1990s at a time when continued economic stagnation was making this ever harder to do. It has also been made plain that, because of the greater difficulty of extracting increased earnings from most businesses under such conditions, higher returns on investment could only be achieved by stimulating a rise in the market valuation of securities through one form of speculation or another. In the long run, however, it would only be possible to sustain such valuations by generating a commensurate rise in the level of profits – or at least a convincing promise that such profit levels would soon be attained. Given the difficulty of reconciling this position with the harsh realities of the marketplace, it was inevitable that an increasing degree of deception had to be deployed by the ruling elite in order to maintain a minimum level of public belief in the soundness of the economic system.

It is, of course, considered more or less normal behaviour for political leaders to resort to shameless exaggeration of the benefits, both actual and projected, of the economic strategies or models they espouse or propose to emulate. Thus the successive 'hyping' of such phenomena as the Japanese and East Asian 'miracles', globalisation and the information technology revolution was evidently regarded as a part of normal political discourse – even by many who may have come to view such visions with scepticism. At the same time most members of the public, who were at least half taken in by these attempts to convince them that there was a crock of gold at the end of the rainbow, probably hardly noticed as each plausible fad proved illusory, only to be replaced by another.

Thus for a long time it was easy for the global corporate establishment, with its dominance over the mass media as well as the Western political leadership, to take advantage of traditionally complacent public opinion. On the other hand it found the task of assuring the stability of the real economy – and of the corporate superstructure on whose health it depended – increasingly problematic. For, as always, the well-being of the system depended on its continued ability to deliver overall growth in corporate profitability. Yet as global economic growth rates in the 1980s and 1990s registered a continuation of the decline begun in 1974–75 it was inevitable that this would ultimately be reflected in a fall-off in the real level of profits.

Just as in the 1970s, however, it was recognised that if the perception of this reality were allowed to take hold in the markets it could only mean that there would be a sustained sell-off of assets such as might lead to a terminal collapse of the entire financial system. Indeed, since stock market values at the end of the 1990s were even more overblown than in the early 1970s (see Table 2.1), the danger of such a cataclysmic crash was even more obvious than twenty-five years earlier. Hence given the ineluctable political commitment to averting such a disaster – or any exposure of the inherent flaws of the capitalist profits system – the compulsion to clutch at any straw was all too understandable. Thus as the fantasies of neoliberalism were remorselessly blown away by successive financial crises in the 1990s, it was perhaps to be expected that those who had hitherto sought salvation through peddling such delusions would now begin to resort to outright fraud.

The limits of manipulation

It has long been an article of faith among the supporters of modern capitalism that the maintenance of confidence in the financial markets is a public good to be highly prized and carefully nurtured. Indeed this view may be said to be central to the Keynesian ideology based on the belief in the desirability of using the resources of the state to bolster the 'animal spirits' of entrepreneurs – a perception also reflected in President Franklin Roosevelt's declaration in 1933 that 'the only thing we have to fear is fear itself'. Judged from this perspective, it may be considered entirely proper that financial institutions and other corporations should be enabled, indeed encouraged, to present their results in the most favourable light possible. By the same token it is entirely rational to promote the development of structures and instruments that help to minimise the danger of systemic financial collapse.

From the 1980s onwards the financial sector has been marked by the development of increasingly ingenious mechanisms for trying to avert such dangers by limiting the exposure of individual businesses to risk. This has taken two principal forms:

- Hedging of risk (e.g. of rising interest rates or a fall in the market value of a currency or commodity) by buying options, futures or other 'derivative' instruments – enabling a company

or investor effectively to take out insurance against such even-
tualities so as to limit their potential losses;
• 'Securitisation' of debt, whereby banks and other lenders can
repackage loans or mortgages into tradable securities (equivalent to bonds), thereby spreading the risk of loss through default among a wide range of investors and institutions.

The apparent success of such 'structured finance' instruments has been reflected in the relative strength and resilience
of the US banking sector in the face of the massive decline
in financial markets generally since 2000 – a source of much
self-congratulation on the part of Chairman Greenspan of the
Federal Reserve Board and other members of the financial establishment.[1] Yet as the depression in the financial markets deepens
it is increasingly obvious that such complacency is hopelessly
misplaced. For while it may be feasible for a limited period to
avert a crisis of confidence in the markets by spreading financial
risk among a large number of institutions, ultimately confidence
can only be maintained if the aggregate level of risk in the
system can be reduced by an improvement in the underlying
economic conditions. Failing this, all that structured finance will
have achieved is to ensure that instead of today's market crash
resulting in a general banking collapse (as in the 1930s) it will be
metamorphosed into a mass collapse of pension funds, insurance
companies and other institutions which have been induced to buy
so many securities of doubtful value.

Indeed there is by now an obvious danger that corporations
that have traditionally been thought of as industrial (or 'non-
financial') will be among the main casualties of market meltdown.
This has become particularly apparent in respect of corporate
defined-benefit pension schemes now that the massive underfund-
ing of these has been revealed in the wake of the stock market

crash (see below). For it has dawned on investors that the balance sheets of the corporations concerned are heavily weighed down by their liabilities under these schemes, which until recently were thought to be net assets as their value was inflated by the market bubble. Hence it has lately become fashionable to refer to Ford and General Motors as pension funds with subsidiaries that make cars, with similar ironic descriptions being applied to British Airways and other corporations with increasing pension fund burdens on their balance sheets. Similarly, the much admired General Electric – in its chronic compulsion to sustain a rapid rate of profit growth through mergers and acquisitions – has arrived at the point where its financial services arm, GE Capital, accounts for over 60 per cent of the group's total book value.

The culture of fraud

While examples of large-scale fraud have punctuated the history of capitalism at least since the days of the great Dutch Tulip Mania of the 1630s, the sheer volume and extent of the financial scandals revealed following the stock market crash of 2000 evidently dwarf anything witnessed since the Industrial Revolution. At the time of writing the full extent of the criminality involved has yet to become clear, especially as there is an evident reluctance on the part of the authorities to bring some of the perpetrators to justice. However, the unfolding financial disaster of the 1990s and beyond has revealed a pattern of deception permeating every sector of the economy, including in particular:

Corporate management As already noted, the pressure on the managers of private-sector companies under capitalism to maintain and increase profitability is inexorable – and become more intense during periods of economic slowdown (the downswing of the business cycle). In a climate where economic stagnation has become chronic (albeit unacknowledged) – while at the same time financial liberalisation and innovative entrepreneurship are extolled as public goods – it is perhaps unsurprising that company chief executives and their henchmen should have taken advantage of the increased scope for misleading investors to engage in large-scale falsification of their accounts. The result was that many companies which had been lauded as the most dynamic exponents of entrepreneurial success in the 1990s – such as Enron, World-Com and Global Crossing – were revealed by the millennium crash as perpetrators of some of the biggest frauds in history. It is obvious, however, that they could not have got away with such crimes for so long – allowing senior executives to pocket vast fortunes at the expense of shareholders, employees and the public at large – without the active complicity of outside bodies (notably auditors) which would normally have been expected to act as a restraint on them.

The banking industry Progressively since the 1970s financial de-regulation has both enabled and encouraged commercial banks to diversify their activities across the whole range of financial services. This relaxation of restrictions imposed on them follow-ing the banking disasters of the 1930s was essentially a response to the increasing squeeze on the profitability of their core busi-ness – that of lending to enterprises.[2] The result has been a radical reshaping of the sector, leading to the emergence of a number of large financial conglomerates, which, in addition to performing the traditional role of deposit taking and lending, now act as stockbrokers and merchant banks, in which capacity they underwrite share issues and advise on mergers and acquisi-tions. Predictably this has led to serious conflicts of interest, in which management have come under pressure to push the sales of the shares of their corporate clients to investors who are unaware of their vested interest in doing so. Since the collapse of the stock market bubble began in March 2000 it has been revealed that senior officials of the world's largest and most respected financial institutions (such as Citigroup, Merrill Lynch and Credit Suisse First Boston) had been engaged in systematic and deliberate lying to their investor clients about the supposedly bright prospects of stocks which they actually considered to be more or less worthless.

Auditors The large-scale frauds now known to have been perpetrated by major corporations during the 1990s boom could not have occurred without the systematic connivance of professional organisations responsible for advising them and monitoring their performance. Of these the accountancy firms responsible for auditing companies' finances – with a fiduciary duty to shareholders – were the most obviously culpable. Yet the existence of conflicts of interest corrupting their professional independence as auditors had been well known for many years. In particular the Big Five global audit partnerships (Arthur Andersen, Deloitte & Touche, Ernst & Young, KPMG and Price Waterhouse Coopers) had increasingly since the 1970s come to generate most of their business from advising companies as consultants – including actual or potential audit clients – on different aspects of their business. This despite the obvious danger of a conflict of interest resulting from their desire to sell their consultancy services to company managers whose performance they were supposed to be monitoring on behalf of shareholders. Although such hazards had long been pointed out, the lobbying power of the audit firms themselves had consistently prevented any official action to curb such abuses – notably heading off a campaign in 1999–2000 by Arthur Levitt, the then chairman of the Securities and Exchange Commission (SEC) – to limit their conflicts of interest. It was not until the Enron scandal (in 2001) exposed the role of Arthur Andersen in actively helping to cook the company's books that governments at last began to make tentative moves to impose some restraints.

Actuaries Although a much less well known profession, this group may turn out to have had as pernicious an influence in facilitating the massive financial perversion of the late twentieth century as the accountants. Traditionally their role has been largely confined to calculating the appropriate level of insurance premiums based on statistical evidence of longevity and other risk factors. More recently, however, they have been called on to put a value on pension funds based on assumptions of future earnings which were supposed to be derived from historic market trends. Applying theoretically objective statistical techniques, they have for long felt able to value corporate pension funds on the assumption that investment returns would be sustained at levels as high as 10–12 per cent for the indefinite future, even though this was known to be three to four times the rate of sustainable economic or earnings growth. The inevitable result of this gross collective betrayal of professional ethics, reinforced by that of the hopelessly conflicted auditors and investment analysts, was to generate enormous exaggeration of the reported net worth not only of the pension funds concerned but of the companies sponsoring them. It thus transpires that supposed corporate assets of hundreds of billions of dollars were actually liabilities.[3]

The extent to which actuaries are now subject to corrupting conflicts of interest is further underlined by revelations that they have systematically and deliberately underestimated longevity in order to justify overvaluing corporate pension funds in order to please their clients, the fund sponsors. Incredibly, US actuaries have even gone so far as to lobby the Pension Benefits Guaranty Corporation to be allowed to assume lower than actual levels of life expectancy for retirees in certain hard-pressed sectors such as airlines in order to boost corporate balance sheets artificially.[4]

Ratings agencies A still more obscure, but highly significant, group of actors in the securities markets are the credit rating agencies, whose judgements on the creditworthiness of corporations (and indeed of national governments) have a great influence on investor sentiment. For in ascribing a rating to a company's debt (at one or other level between 'investment grade' and 'junk') these agencies play a large part in determining the values placed by the market on both bonds and equities, and can thus in certain circumstances have the power to decide whether companies live or die. This point was painfully brought home to investors at the time of the Enron collapse – when both the major agencies were still awarding the company's debt an investment grade rating. This focused attention on the fact that the credit rating business – which is largely unregulated and an effective duopoly of two private sector US companies (Moody's Investors Service and Standard & Poor's) – was seriously lacking in transparency and potentially subject to conflicts of interest similar to those of accountants.

Stock markets Since the 1980s stock exchanges have increasingly been transformed – with the full blessing of the authorities – from staid quasi-public institutions owned and managed as mutual (i.e. non-profit) organisations into profit-maximising corporations. They have also grown in number – largely thanks to the advance of technology, which has made it possible for trading to be carried on electronically and without the need for substantial investment in large buildings. The effect has been to encourage increasing competition for business both within and across national boundaries. This in turn has led to yet another race to the bottom in terms of standard setting, as exchanges have lowered the listing requirements demanded in order to maximise the number of listed companies and thus, it is hoped, the volume of trade. Hence whereas in the past companies could only get access to the liquidity of public stock markets after demonstrating a track record of profits over some years, it has now become possible on many exchanges to gain a listing almost from the moment a company opens for business.[5] Obviously this new laxity was an essential feature of the permissive climate of the 1990s, enabling large numbers of dotcom companies that had never made a profit (providing such commodities as pet food via the Internet) to offer their shares to a gullible investing public.

For mainstream economists and commentators, who spent the last two decades of the twentieth century extolling the virtues of the capitalist free market, this catalogue of abuse and systemic failure has naturally caused huge ideological difficulty. Forced to come up with an explanation of what has happened, they have almost unanimously put the blame on the 'corruption' and 'greed' of a managerial class intoxicated by the opportunities for self-enrichment in a climate of deregulation and unbridled individualism.[6] The reality that none of the system's apologists has felt able to confront is that this phenomenon was largely the inevitable consequence of the unrelenting pressure to sustain or increase profits in a competitive climate where this was becoming ever harder, combined with the pernicious influence of moral hazard. The deep-rooted nature of this weakened ethical sense is revealed in such phenomena as

- The widespread incidence of overcharging and trading malpractice (at the expense of investors) revealed in the SEC's investigation – begun in 2003 – of the mammoth US mutual fund industry. (Such tendencies are all the easier to understand in view of the combination of (a) the tax breaks cushioning investors and thus encouraging the complacent feeling that they could be sure of reasonable returns without the need to be particularly vigilant, and (b) the typical opacity of the funds' charging structures).

- The unashamed demand of the British venture capital industry, amidst the wreckage of the post-crash markets, for still greater tax breaks in the interests of encouraging the 'enterprise culture'.[7]

Yet the still more fearful truth that dare not speak its name is that such behaviour is the expression of the establishment's compulsive commitment never to confront the reality of the inescapable business cycle. It is this fundamental denial – for which the compelling rationale is described in earlier chapters – that lies behind virtually all the economic crimes and misdemeanours of the capitalist establishment in the late twentieth century.

Complicity of the state

This massive betrayal of ethical standards and fiduciary obligations by the groups entrusted with maintaining faith in self-regulated capitalism could hardly have occurred without the active connivance of the authorities that are supposed to be accountable to the public for assuring economic stability. This is most obviously true of the whole process of financial deregulation, which, as we have seen, served not only to create increasing conflicts of interest, scope for market manipulation and covert subsidy mechanisms – see Chapter 3 – but also to facilitate concealment of the myriad resulting abuses. More fundamentally, however, the authority and resources of the state have increasingly been hijacked by the private sector to serve their interests at the expense of society as a whole. This is most conspicuously apparent in phenomena such as:

The great pensions fraud   The development of funded pension schemes (heavily invested in corporate stocks) as the main source of retirement income in the United States and other countries has been a unique feature of capitalism over the last half century. As noted in Chapter 1, it has been implicitly recognised since the early 1970s (at least in the United States) that it is an inherently insecure system which could hardly remain viable in face of a prolonged downturn in the markets typical of the normal business cycle. Yet not only has there been no official attempt to discourage or phase out reliance on such schemes as their unsustainability has become apparent; their scale has actually been greatly extended with the full authority and blessing of governments. Thus tax incentives have been deployed to encourage still greater investment of retirement savings in such schemes – as with so-called 401(k) schemes in the USA – while there have been moves in both the USA and Britain to reduce reliance on safer pay-as-you-go state schemes in favour of committing contributions to funded schemes instead.[8] Given the enormous and increasingly obvious danger that funded schemes would ultimately be unable to meet their obligations, the fact that reliance on them was fostered by governments clearly means the latter were accessories to their fraudulent promotion by Wall Street and the City. (Even more astoundingly, in Britain the Trades Union Congress has allowed itself to be co-opted into demanding that all working people should be legally compelled to subscribe to such schemes – apparently without even any guarantee of a minimum pension at the end.) Meanwhile, of course, the only victims of this officially authorized fraud have been the millions of pensioners exposed to ruin since the start of the millennium market crash and those taxpayers called on to subsidise the industry both through massive tax breaks (worth some £14 billion a year in Britain) and bail-outs of failed schemes. (In fact, given the huge volume of money by now accumulated in pension funds, it may appear that they have degenerated into a giant subsidized share buying scheme, in which corporations receive tax incentives to buy each other's stock at ever more inflated prices).

The false prospectus of privatisation   Contrary to official propaganda, profit-driven enterprises have proved unable to deliver essential public services on a secure, cost-effective basis – as demonstrated by the performance failures and increasing financial fragility of, inter alia, health care providers in the USA, power suppliers in the USA and Britain and, most notably, Britain's fragmented railways. Instead privatisation has thrown up countless instances of corruption and waste at the expense of both taxpayers and consumers – on a scale that has become increasingly apparent since the late 1990s. Indeed a number of such instances have made it appear that privatisation is almost synonymous with the theft of public assets – just as much as the corruption and embezzlement of Third World dictators such as former Presidents Marcos and Mobutu. Among the more egregious cases have been

- the underpricing of privatised assets (e.g. the sale of the rolling stock of British Rail in 1996 at a price far below its market value, thus enabling the purchasers to make a speculative profit of hundreds of millions of pounds on reselling them);
- fraudulent claims running to billions of dollars by US pharmaceuticals manufacturers and private health care firms at the expense of federal programmes such as Medicare and Medicaid

(involving, in one instance, performing unnecessary heart operations);[9]

- the covert burdening of taxpayers with the extra costs of private provision of public services – as in the case of contracts under Britain's Private Finance Initiative (PFI) where, contrary to official propaganda, the risk of cost overruns has often been left with the government instead of being transferred to the contractor, while at the same time the terms of PFI deals have often been so generous to the private contractors that they have been able to make a speculative profit by selling their stakes in contracts to other operators.[10]

Bankruptcy: a perverted process? Just as state bail-outs of financial institutions and non-financial corporations have weakened the market discipline that is supposed to ensure that economic resources are allocated efficiently under capitalism, so there is also a sign that the watering down of bankruptcy procedures is giving an added dimension to moral hazard, especially in the United States. It is of course a familiar peril of the limited liability system that it creates the potential for fraudulent bankruptcy – a criminal offence whereby the owners of a company deliberately make it bankrupt in order to steal from their creditors. From the 1980s, however, it has become the conventional wisdom in the USA that the bankruptcy regulations should be made sufficiently flexible to ensure that inherently viable businesses are not put into liquidation to the possible detriment of the public interest – e.g. through large-scale loss of jobs. This has encouraged the growing practice in the USA of financially troubled companies seeking protection from their creditors under Chapter 11 of the Bankruptcy Code. This allows a debtor to seek a restructuring of the company in a way that enables it to emerge from bankruptcy as a going concern while, in principle, ensuring that its creditors receive at

least as much as they would have got in the event of liquidation.
Although this may seem a justifiable practice in 'normal' economic
times, in the crisis-ridden conditions of the new century it has
been revealed as a potential vehicle for evasion of liabilities. In
fact Chapter 11 bankruptcy has become a mechanism for financial
institutions effectively to avoid writing off bad loans by agreeing
to the relaunch of a failed company in which they retain most of
their original investment (as loan or equity) on the pretext that it
is a potentially viable business. Increasingly, however, this process
is being recognised as serving to perpetuate excess capacity in
many sectors where theoretically market forces would dictate the
need for a shakeout – notably in the air transport, steel, energy
and telecommunications sectors. The result is the 'zombification'
(see Chapter 1) of an increasing number of enterprises in these
sectors and consequent postponement of economic recovery just
as has occurred in Japan since 1990.[11]

Rape of the emerging markets   As noted in Chapter 2, Third World
countries that were once regarded as too unattractive and risky to
justify significant investment by serious Western enterprises have
in recent years been encouraged (not least by the IMF and the
World Bank) to open up to foreign capital. By the late 1990s, however, successive financial crises in Mexico, East Asia and Russia
had demonstrated not only that investors' traditional scepticism
about such markets was largely justified, but that the inflow of
largely speculative funds had done lasting damage to many of the
countries concerned – by destabilising their currencies and financial systems. What virtually nobody has recognised is the extent
to which this destructive process has been encouraged by the US
authorities and the IMF in particular. This they did both by tacitly
guaranteeing the loans of US investors in Mexico (through the
massive bail-out launched by the Clinton administration in 1995)

and by the often corrupt encouragement of unaffordable borrowing by countries such as Russia (as well as other former Soviet
republics) and, most spectacularly, by Argentina. Indeed the latter
initiatives should be seen as an officially orchestrated criminal
conspiracy to induce chronically weak economies to issue debt
at unsustainably high interest rates, thereby permitting Western
speculators and financial institutions to make super-profits – as
long as the IMF obligingly propped up the local exchange rate
against the dollar. Such an approach, it may be noted, is indeed
strikingly similar to that of 'loan-sharking' – a traditional activity
of organised crime all over the world. (At the time of writing the
extent of this scandal has escaped the attention of the Western
media, perhaps because the cost to taxpayers in industrialised
countries has been relatively small. In contrast it has contributed
greatly to mass impoverishment in Russia, Argentina and elsewhere – all the more so because the resulting high real interest
rates have crippled the development of local enterprise.[12])

Perhaps no other single instance of abuse of power by Western
governments better demonstrates the extent of their betrayal of
public trust than this systematic, criminal assault on the welfare
of the world's poorest and most vulnerable communities in the
interests of organised capital. For a while it might have seemed
possible to believe that the imposition of the destructive Washington consensus across the globe was simply the result of misguided
and overzealous ideologues. On the other hand there is ample evidence that senior officials of the World Bank and the IMF were
fully aware that their support for such extreme liberalisation was
contrary to the interests of the countries concerned. A notable
example was Stanley Fischer, who served both institutions in high
positions in the 1980s and 1990s. Thus in 1991 he wrote in a World
Bank paper, 'financial liberalisation is extremely risky unless a

sound system of accounting, auditing, prudential regulation and supervision is in place and unless the macroeconomy is reasonable stable',[13] – before going on to impose just such unwise liberalisation on the most vulnerable and unreformed ex-Communist countries in his capacity as vice-president of the IMF.

By the late 1990s, however, following the successive financial crises in Mexico, East Asia and Russia, it was no longer possible to plead ignorance of the ruin that was being inflicted on the people of economically weak countries exposed to uncontrolled market forces in an increasingly anarchic world order. Such were the obvious contradictions that in 1999 a prominent member of the international establishment, Joseph Stiglitz, then the World Bank's chief economist, finally felt compelled to denounce the strategy of extreme liberalisation imposed on the former Soviet Union in particular.[14] It can hardly be doubted that this commendable frankness, which cost Stiglitz his job, was driven by his genuine remorse at the suffering visited on poor countries by the Washington consensus. Yet the idea that the imposition of such strategies may have been driven by criminal interests as much as by ideological perversion is one that probably did not occur to him.

Many more examples can be cited of official readiness to aid and abet more or less criminal acts by big business, as the pressures to avert corporate collapse or financial meltdown have increasingly come in conflict with the demands of the law. Two cases that came to light at the end of 2003 illustrate the still powerful tendency to turn an official blind eye to corporate wrongdoing even in the aftermath of the Enron and other scandals which had supposedly induced a determination on the part of the establishment to restore public faith in the integrity of capitalism.

- *Systematic fraud in the British mortgage market* Revelations by the BBC have exposed the widespread practice among mortgage lenders of inciting borrowers to overstate their incomes (by 100 per cent or more) on application forms to obtain housing loans. As a result many have been enabled to borrow up to 10 times their income (compared with a normal maximum of 3–4 times), convinced that they can afford the repayments at a time of exceptionally low interest rates. Despite the fact that this well-publicised practice clearly constitutes fraud (a criminal offence) – and has also contributed to a dangerously unsustainable inflation of real-estate prices – the regulatory authorities have taken no action to stamp it out.[15]

• *Parmalat – Europe's Enron*   When it was disclosed in December 2003 that the Italian-based food multinational had a €4 billion hole in its balance sheet, it first appeared that this was a simple case of theft by the group's top management. However, it subsequently emerged that a significant part of the company's losses (accumulated over thirty years) resulted from political favours provided to government leaders around the world (such as acquiring loss-making state-owned milk-processing plants). The clear implication is that the absorption of such losses in the public interest might be regarded by the authorities as somehow rendering a degree of false accounting acceptable.[16]

Both cases exemplify the pernicious influence that moral hazard has come to exert on the entire economic system through the official identification of private corporate interests with the public interest. It should be noted, moreover, that even though the actions of the authorities in these cases might *a priori* have been justifiable from a public interest perspective, in practice the lack of transparency and conflict of interest resulted in massive damage to taxpayers, consumers, employees and shareholders alike.

As suggested earlier, all these symptoms of malfeasance and disregard for public welfare at the highest levels of both business and government cannot be ascribed to mere moral degeneracy – nor to the increasing opportunities for criminal infiltration of economic structures permeated by moral hazard. They are above all the product of efforts to keep intact an economic system based predominantly on self-regulated, profit-maximising capitalism in face of pressures which have rendered such a system progressively more unworkable. If the fraud and deception perpetrated in pursuit of this objective are on a scale unseen in the previous history of capitalism, this is primarily because (as already noted) the only alternative ways of resolving the crisis are seen to be absolutely unacceptable to the ruling establishment itself. At the same time, however, the legitimisation of moral hazard since World War II has undoubtedly blinded many corporate and government leaders to the dangers of some of their actions – and may help to explain why so many seem unable to recognise a conflict of interest when confronted with one. A frightening illustration of the extent to which the some of the most exalted figures of the establishment have lost any kind of ethical compass is provided by the conduct of Robert Rubin, former US treasury secretary (in the Clinton administration) during the Enron collapse in 2001. Having joined the financial conglomerate Citigroup on his departure from Washington, he felt no compunction in seeking (unsuccessfully) to persuade the Bush administration to use taxpayers' money to bail out Enron – of which Citigroup was a major creditor – notwithstanding the obvious evidence of wrongdoing.[17]

A similarly corrosive consequence of the combining of Keynesian corporatist attitudes with those of neoliberal individualism has been the spreading contempt for the state in much of the industrialised world since the 1970s. This syndrome may be seen as reflecting both the intense ideological crusade in favour of private enterprise – begetting consequent denigration of public ownership – and the perception nevertheless that the state can and should be called on to bail out and subsidise private businesses. The net result was to create a general tendency to regard the state and the public sector as 'fair game' – to be robbed and at the same time used – without any thought of the long-term damage that might flow from this lack of concern to protect public assets and resources.[18] Even now that major global companies have discovered the virtues of 'corporate social responsibility', while continuing to evade tax worldwide on an ever-increasing scale,[19] the contradictions of such attitudes are scarcely perceived.

These tendencies demonstrate clearly that, so far from the corporate elite showing signs of greater social responsibility (as they are being urged to do in the post-Enron climate of capitalist soul-searching), they have become more and more irresponsible in their desperate pursuit of survival. Nowhere is this more frighteningly obvious than in their reckless disregard for the long-term security of the state and public patrimony, referred to above. At the same time their willingness to lay waste many of the world's most disadvantaged countries in pursuit of short-term speculative gain (with the full connivance of pillars of the international system such as the IMF) bespeaks a global establishment utterly bereft of any sense of morality. The potentially devastating consequences of this syndrome as the crisis deepens are addressed in Chapter 6.

5

A System Past Reforming

It is a striking fact that in the space of little more than ten years since the early 1990s the public image of the global capitalist economic order has been transformed from that of an almost universally triumphant success to one of chaotic failure bordering on collapse. Although the powerful propaganda machine of the ruling vested interests has partly succeeded in blurring the public's perception of the full extent of this systemic crisis, there are unmistakable signs not only of breakdown in the functioning of global capitalism but of rising discontent with it. The principal symptoms of this malaise may be summarised as follows:

The collapse in global stock markets   By the middle of 2003 this had wiped out about $13 trillion in market capitalisation worldwide[1] (equivalent to around 40 per cent of global GDP) since the start of the crash in March 2000. Moreover, given that stocks are on average (at least in the USA) scarcely less overvalued than they were on the eve of the crash in December 1999, they clearly have much further to fall – notwithstanding the market rally that saw values recover by over 30 per cent between March and December 2003. Although at the time of writing the worst effects of this disaster have been kept at bay by a drastic easing of credit orchestrated by the US Federal Reserve and other central banks, it is already clear that the consequences are potentially far more severe than was the case in any previous crash. The reason for this is that, unlike earlier market collapses such as that of 1929–31, the financial well-being of the mass of individual citizens (particularly in the Anglo-Saxon countries) is now directly linked to the performance of the financial markets through publicly subsidised funded pension schemes. The resulting threat to the retirement incomes of so many is a social and political problem of potentially catastrophic proportions.

Crisis of confidence in the corporate and financial establishment This has become particularly associated with the collapse of Enron and other fraudulently run companies starting in 2001. Yet it is also linked in the public consciousness with more general failures of corporate governance manifested in such abuses as excessive rewards for top executives (including those who have presided over disasters) and mis-selling of investment products to the general public.

The emergence of active anti-capitalist/anti-globalisation movements General discontent at chronic world poverty, rising inequality, damage to the environment and other manifestations of economic and social dysfunction has crystallised since the late 1990s in growing mass demonstrations of opposition to the status quo. (Arguably this phenomenon may also be partly connected with the virtual collapse of civil order and the authority of the state in an increasing number of Third World countries – even if this is not necessarily recognised as being a specific symptom of capitalist failure.)

Such unmistakable signs of actual or potential breakdown have compelled the authorities to respond with some kind of remedial action – or at least to try and give the appearance of doing so. This is more than an exercise in political damage limitation. For without some gesture towards restoring belief in the integrity of the system – and in its capacity to deliver benefits to the mass of investors, as well as the general public – a continuing rapid plunge in stock markets towards total 'meltdown' would have been virtually guaranteed. Likewise the destruction of what little public respect the corporate sector still retains – if not the total discrediting of the capitalist system – would have been assured, with potentially grave political consequences.

An exercise in cosmetics

Inevitably, however, the measures that have been taken to date have been largely symbolic. This is because, as we have observed in earlier chapters, most if not all of the manifestations of dishonesty and other market abuses which had so damaged public confidence were caused by ferocious pressures to deliver investment returns that have become increasingly unattainable in the prevailing economic conditions. Hence the numerous measures that have been proposed or enacted in order to improve corporate governance or tighten the regulation of financial markets are bound to prove either empty gestures of a purely cosmetic nature or else only implementable at the cost of further depressing the markets and the economy.

Strengthening corporate governance The need to devise ways of making companies more accountable to their shareholders (their ultimate owners) has been an issue of public concern at various

times throughout the last two hundred years – indeed at least
since Adam Smith decried the very idea of joint stock companies
in 1776.[2] Since the 1980s, however, public concern over corporate
governance has been aroused not only by the lack of effective
accountability to shareholders – who now represent the interests
of millions of small investors through pension and mutual funds
– but by awareness of the enormous and growing power of corporations to affect economic and social conditions in an increasingly deregulated world. Yet despite a number of official inquiries
into the subject, notably in Britain, little has been done to change
the reality of centralised and unaccountable corporate power
beyond the drafting of a few innocuous codes of practice.

With the advent of the millennium crash and the subsequent
exposure of endemic financial fraud on an unimagined scale, the
demand for more concrete action has suddenly become inescapable. However, thus far the only resulting legislation to occur
anywhere has been the Sarbanes–Oxley Act passed in the USA
in 2002, the most drastic provision of which is to make company
chief executives personally guarantee the truthfulness of their
published accounts – with the possibility of jail terms for vio-
lators. It is clearly hoped that by such measures it will be possible
to reassure the investing public that a corner has been turned and
that accounting abuses by companies and their auditors will be
severely punished. Yet otherwise this hastily drafted legislation
makes only the most feeble gestures towards making auditors
more independent of the chief executives of the companies
they audit, including proposals to mandate the rotation of audit
companies every few years – despite the lack of any evidence
that this could be beneficial.[3]

Making investors responsible In theory another way of rendering
corporate governance more effective is to induce shareholders

themselves to be more vigilant and proactive in their oversight of management. Since the 1980s support for this approach has come from an increasingly vocal shareholder activist movement (backed by some of the largest public-sector pension funds in the USA). It has even received official backing from American regulatory authorities such as the SEC, which are supporting the view that investors should be required to vote on key aspects of top executives' remuneration and that independent directors (i.e. not nominated by the chief executive or existing directors) should constitute a majority of the board.

The very fact that shareholder activism is ostensibly taken seriously by such pillars of the capitalist establishment can be regarded as confirmation of the essential hollowness of the whole movement for corporate governance reform. For the practical obstacles to making it effective are essentially the same as those that troubled Adam Smith in the eighteenth century and have remained familiar ever since,[4] namely that

- it is impossible for shareholders or their proxies who are not engaged in the day-to-day management of a company (outsiders) to have as much knowledge of its needs as the directors who are paid to manage it (insiders);
- it is more cost-effective for shareholders seeking to maximise their return on investment to sell the shares of companies whose performance they find unsatisfactory than to try and improve it, since the latter course can be costly and uncertain in its outcome.

If anything these constraints are even greater in the contemporary capitalist environment in which the main shareholders tend to be fund management institutions which are themselves under competitive pressure to deliver optimal returns to their investor clients (such as company pension funds). For this reality puts in particularly stark relief the daunting obstacle to shareholder activism posed by the problem of the 'free rider'. This refers to the inescapable fact that the benefits of activism by one share-holder – in terms of improved returns – are shared equally by all shareholders, whether they have incurred the costs of activism or not. Hence it is inevitable that the most successful fund managers – that is, the ones delivering the highest returns – will be those least engaged in shareholder activism. Indeed this seems to be borne out by the fact that the most high-profile shareholder activist funds in the USA tend to be those large public-sector ones such as the California Public Employees Retirement System (CALPERS) which are not subject to the same commercial pressures as private-sector ones. The position of the latter is typified by the statement of the head of Citigroup's fund management arm in 2003 that 'I'm not a do-gooder. I want to do what I get paid for, and shareholder activism isn't what I get paid for.'[5] Given such understandable attitudes, it seems unlikely that compelling investors to vote on executive remuneration packages will make any meaningful difference to such decisions.

Investor education: an exercise in absurdity   One of the more bizarre features of financial settlements reached since 2001 between US regulators and major securities firms found to have wilfully misled investors is the inclusion in the compensation package of hundreds of millions of dollars to be dedicated to educating ordinary investors. Similar proposals for enhanced investor education – to enable the man in the street to select savings and investment products more wisely – have been advanced in Britain. Few commentators seem to have noticed the irony in thus proposing that securities firms – a central part of whose activities is to talk up the attractions of investment products while obscuring the risks – should undertake to instruct their customers on how to see through their own salesmen's patter. In fact behind this idea there seems to be an implicit suggestion, naturally popular with fund managers, that small investors who lost their savings and pensions in the market debacle have only themselves to blame for buying products whose risks they did not understand – and hence for their own downfall. Yet clearly this fails to take account of the reality that the vast majority of small investors have neither the time nor the capacity to become financial experts and must depend on others to guide them through the market minefield. This point is all the more valid for those who are forced to save for their retirement individually by the increasing inadequacy of state or company pension schemes. For such people the notion that they should be better equipped to provide for their old age by training them as professional investors is about as rational as proposing that they should be encouraged to study medicine in order to improve their health. Moreover, even if they were to be so trained it is clear that they would be no better placed than the average fund manager to predict the timing and scale of the next market crash.

Cleaning up the accounts? A central feature of the scandalous corporate financial failures witnessed in the wake of the millennium market crash has been the huge scale of false accounting involved. Moreover, as noted in the last chapter, this has generally happened with the full endorsement, if not active encouragement, of the supposedly independent auditors whose duty it was to prevent it. The conviction of one of the Big Five audit groups, Arthur Andersen, in 2002 for obstruction of justice in relation to the Enron collapse (a rare example of the successful criminal prosecution of a corporate entity) is only the most spectacular example of the auditing profession's fall from grace. Yet with massive claims for damages outstanding against the surviving major audit firms, the crisis in the profession is far from over. In the United States the perceived need for remedial action has prompted the creation of a federal government regulator, the Public Company Accounting Oversight Board, in place of the traditional system of self-regulation. At the same time a number of restrictions have been imposed with a view to removing conflicts of interest, notably the curtailment of firms' ability to offer consultancy services to the companies they audit – something the profession had successfully lobbied against for years before the crash.

In reality, however, there seems little prospect that such changes will succeed in enhancing the independence of auditors from the senior management of companies that they audit, given the likelihood that their appointment will continue to depend on the goodwill of the latter and of the board of directors. Moreover, even if, as recently proposed in Britain, company audit committees (responsible for appointing the auditors) were composed mainly of independent directors, it seems probable that the strong symbiotic links between many directors and one or other of the Big Four[6] will tend to compromise the auditors' independence.[7] At the same time, given the continuing strong incentives for management to maximise short-term shareholder value by all available means – and the probably minimal impact of independent directors in restraining them – it must be expected that the race to the bottom in accounting standards will continue (see below).

Perhaps even more fatal in the long run to any prospect of restoring faith in the reliability of company accounts will be the changing nature of capital assets and hence of the basis for valuing companies (see Chapter 2). As is now widely recognised, this is tending to make accountancy still less of a science and more of an art than ever, thus increasing the scope for 'creative' accounting in the valuation process.

Inescapable pressures of the market

In the light of the earlier analysis of how the global economy has sunk into its present state of turmoil, it is not hard to see why the current moves to reform capitalist institutions in the wake of the recent systemic disasters outlined above are doomed to be ineffective. For one thing above all is clear: that if it were possible for such reforms to be genuinely implemented, the effect would be to reduce the profitability of enterprises – both financial and non-financial – in both real and apparent terms, since obviously (a) the costs of compliance with the new rules would impose a net reduction in the overall operating margin of businesses, and (b) the scope for inflating the level of reported profits would be significantly curtailed. It follows that the current market value of most corporate securities would appear even more excessive relative to earnings than it does already, making a further catastrophic slide in stock markets inevitable. Since it goes without saying that such a prospect is too awful for the global establishment to contemplate, it is safe to assume that all official talk of the institutional reform of capitalism is mere lip-service.

In the real, hard-headed world of intensifying competitive struggle – against a background of dwindling opportunities for making genuine profits – few corporate leaders can doubt the need for continued duplicity in describing their financial performance to the investing public. Thus, while tighter regulation of auditing might in future help to curb some of the more outrageous frauds on the scale of Enron, there seems no reason to doubt that corporate management and securities traders will still enjoy plentiful opportunities to present financial results in a deceptively favourable light to investors, most of whom have neither the inclination, nor even in many cases the ability, to analyse the published accounts themselves. Moreover, institutional investors, who will still be the dominant force within the share-buying community, will be as much as ever driven by considerations of short-term performance indicators rather than of the long-term solvency of the funds they manage. Hence they will remain all too willing to be seduced by the latest technique for putting 'spin' on results employed by both corporate management and stock-promoting analysts eager to talk up the value of shares to the market. Such devices tend to include putting emphasis on

- so-called 'proforma earnings' (typically excluding the effect of certain costs claimed to be exceptional); or
- 'earnings before interest, tax, depreciation and amortisation' (EBITDA), a formula notionally designed to give a fairer picture of the financial position of companies engaged in high levels of capital spending or acquisition of other businesses (and whose underlying profitability would allegedly be distorted by including interest, depreciation and other charges).

While such euphemistic devices may by now have been discredited in the eyes of many,[8] leading quoted companies remain largely unrestrained in their use of them to lift the market rating of their shares. Thus the online bookseller Amazon.com, which notoriously has never made a profit in strict accounting terms, nevertheless managed to report proforma earnings of $42 million in the second quarter of 2003, thereby beating analysts' (alleged) expectations and sending the share price up 15 per cent.[9] (This example, it may be noted, illustrates the effective collusion between quoted companies and investing institutions to inflate the value of stocks.) Hence for all the rhetoric about enhancing the integrity and transparency of corporate accounts, it is clear there is a general resolve among the financial establishment that the hyperbole has to continue.

The price of accountability

Another fundamental conflict between the rhetoric of reforming corporate governance and compelling capitalist reality is the difficulty in imposing meaningful deterrents to corporate wrongdoing without seriously inhibiting the willingness of managers to take risks in pursuit of profit maximisation. When such claims are made by business leaders they may often seem to be no more than self-serving propaganda. Yet further reflection should suggest that the exposure of corporate executives to the possibility of penalties involving either personal bankruptcy or imprisonment could indeed potentially discourage the most able and motivated individuals from accepting positions of executive responsibility.

This problem is most pointedly raised by the key provision of the US Sarbanes–Oxley Act of 2002 mandating criminal penalties for chief executives signing off company accounts which are subsequently found to contain false information. For it is quite easy to envisage that this could happen as a result of errors (deliberate or not) by others, which the chief executive was not in a position to identify but would nonetheless be held responsible for. In order to minimise this danger it would very likely be necessary to change the whole corporate ethos from one of supposedly dynamic and creative profit maximisation in a highly competitive environment to one of extreme caution and emphasis on preserving the value of the company through minimal risk taking.

Any such tendencies could, moreover, be seen as moving away from the principle of limited liability which has been regarded as the bedrock of capitalist enterprise – at least in the Anglo-Saxon world – since the mid-Victorian era. If taken seriously and sustained across the world's market economies for any significant period, this would seem bound to mean much more restricted scope for competition and even lower levels of profit than at present. The implications for stock market values, in both the short and the long run, are obvious – as are those for the survival of capitalism based on the voluntary investment of private money in enterprises.

Hence it follows that if the tightening up of corporate governance is to be effective enough to make management behave responsibly in the interests of shareholders – not to mention the rest of society – it risks 'killing the goose that lays the golden egg' by severely weakening its essential dynamic. On the other hand it is clearly not tenable to leave the existing structures of self-regulation untouched in the wake of such an unprecedented epidemic of corporate fraud and malfeasance. Indeed to do so would obviously be at least as damaging to the survival prospects of the capitalist profits system as it is suggested any truly effective governance reform measures would be.

It is plausible to suppose that growing awareness of such contradictory pressures is already leading some entrepreneurs to seek a way out from the market while taking as much accumulated corporate value with them as they can. This may, for example, explain the growing tendency of company boards to vote themselves (along with their chief executives) higher rewards even in the face of declining corporate profitability – to the obvious detriment of their company's long-term survival prospects. It may also account for the reported moves by the family-dominated board of Sainsbury's (the British supermarket giant) to extract over £100 million in dividends from the struggling company in 2003 in anticipation of what they evidently saw as the welcome prospect of a takeover bid.[10] (Such methods of siphoning off funds may perhaps be seen as the legal approach to achieving the same objective as that of the perpetrators of spectacular frauds such as those of Enron and Parmalat already referred to.)

Similar contradictions bedevil attempts to make the audit profession more accountable. In Britain, for example, the prospect that huge claims for damages relating to the Enron and other scandals might put senior partners of the Big Four audit firms into bankruptcy has led to demands for them to be granted limited liability. This again highlights the dilemma facing the whole system. For if this proposal were accepted it would clearly tend to weaken rather then strengthen the profession's accountability. On the other hand, if it were not accepted there is a clear danger that accountants would tend to refuse audit work. Faced with this conundrum governments may ultimately reach the conclusion that auditing is a function which should properly be carried out by non-profit public-sector organisations, based on a scale of charges which would reflect the fact that the state was bearing the full liability for any errors or wrongdoing. (A similar verdict seems inescapable on the future of the equally conflicted actuaries and ratings agencies – see Chapter 4.)

For the present, not surprisingly, such radical solutions to the dilemma of corporate accountability are far from being on the agenda. Instead, it is clearly the official hope that exhortation and threats of severe penalties will at least convince the public that corporations are under effective pressure to behave more responsibly. Yet the actual penalties imposed on deviant companies – often without the offenders being prosecuted or even having to admit wrongdoing – are typically fines that are trivial in relation to the wealth of the organisations concerned and naturally bear on the shareholders as a whole rather than any particularly culpable individual. Moreover, as noted earlier in relation to the recent frauds pertaining to US health-care programmes (see Chapter 4), penalties often do not even result in any restriction on the miscreants continuing to supply the same markets as before. Hence one may reasonably conclude that, as noted in a leading US business journal, there is a risk that the penalties, however large, will be treated simply as a cost of doing business rather than as a meaningful deterrent.[11]

Another indicator of the true level of official sincerity in respect of corporate wrongdoing is the absence of any recognition of the need to remove the incentives for conflict of interest which have been wilfully introduced by the authorities since the early 1980s. This is particularly evident in the failure to propose any reversal of the process of financial deregulation. This is all the more striking given that many of the regulations that have been abandoned were precisely the ones, such as the US Glass–Steagall Act of 1933 concerning the activities of banks, which were originally enacted to prevent a recurrence of the malfeasance surrounding the 1929 crash and its aftermath.

The stakeholder myth

Another fantastic notion with which some would-be rescuers of capitalism would seek to entertain a sceptical public is that private-sector corporations can somehow be made to behave more responsibly by encouraging them to give less priority to profit maximisation and more to wider social concerns such as employment. In theory this would entail giving some form of representation in corporate management to 'stakeholder' groups (particularly employees and consumers) alongside that of shareholders. Yet although this idea enjoyed a considerable vogue in the 1990s, attempts to make it a reality have either not materialised or have been (as in the United States) a demonstrable failure.

That such an outcome has been completely predictable is yet another indicator of the desperation felt by the system's apologists in searching for a new set of clothes in which to dress the naked emperor – even at the cost of abandoning all intellectual self-respect. For it should be obvious that no device for representing non-shareholder interests in corporate decision-taking can be genuinely effective without challenging the primacy of property rights – a fundamental principle of capitalism. It therefore comes as no surprise at all that it has proved impossible to devise a mechanism for giving stakeholders a voice on company boards that does not leave ultimate power as much with the directors (if not with the chief executive alone) as it was before. Indeed it is a grotesque irony that in the USA – the one country where there has been a significant attempt to apply the principle (through the introduction of so-called stakeholder laws in most states) – the main effect of such measures has been, paradoxically, to strengthen the power of chief executives. For these laws have enabled them to justify taking decisions (such as to resist a takeover by another company), which are in their own personal interests but against those of shareholders – on the grounds that they will protect stakeholders (e.g. as employees), even though there was no objective basis for taking account of the latter's interests.[12]

In this survey of the cosmetic half-measures and bogus stratagems being deployed to try to neutralise rising popular hostility to corporate power it is notable that one common theme emerges. This is the struggle to reconcile justifiable public concerns with the overriding capitalist imperative of keeping self-regulated corporate power intact. Yet it has also been shown that ultimately this struggle is futile and that the two objectives are incompatible. For it is unmistakably clear that entrepreneurs and investors can only achieve competitive returns in a chronically stagnant economy if they are allowed to take risks in a lightly regulated market. In such an environment it is virtually inevitable that there will be conflicts of interest and that the playing field will be far from level. By the same token it must be obvious that all talk of the

need for 'corporate social responsibility' – as of making companies accountable to so-called stakeholders – is nothing but the
emptiest rhetoric and purest humbug.

It is thus possible to agree with many supporters of the system
who argue that trying to run a completely clean capital market
may restrict fraud but will also lead to a loss of dynamism by
restricting flows of information and hence efficient investment.[13]
In truth such an insight is far from new. Thus, for example, it has
long been argued by many that it is inappropriate to criminalise
insider dealing – that is, buying and selling shares on the basis of
privileged information not generally available in the market – on
the grounds that gaining access to restricted, market-sensitive information is the very essence of the securities trading business.

If this not unreasonable view is accepted it follows that a
certain degree of distortion, fraud, inequity and conflict of interest must be seen as a virtually inescapable concomitant of any
dynamic model of capitalism. However, for such dubious consequences to be acceptable to the public there must clearly be a
trade-off. This must take the form of an economic and financial
system which is capable of delivering adequate levels of income
and economic welfare to the vast majority of the population
– both before and after retirement – on a sustainable basis. It
is precisely the inability of modern capitalism to deliver such
minimum benefits – even while it continues to facilitate financial
wrongdoing on a scale without historical precedent – which must
surely call its survival into question.

Indeed for all the justified cynicism over existing official proposals to improve corporate governance, the pressures for such
change could well turn out to be harbingers of an irreversible
trend towards greater accountability and the ending of self-
regulation. This may be all the more politically acceptable to
the extent that public opinion finds itself less and less able to

see any general benefit from the private profit motive. It is thus increasingly hard to see how the protagonists of capitalism can possibly reconcile the intensifying contradictions identified in this chapter. As will be shown in the next chapter, their only hope seems to be the slender one that they can maintain a plausible belief in the prospect of spontaneous economic and financial recovery while trying to placate public opinion in the meantime with some superficial gestures towards corporate reform.

6

No End to Denial

A recurring theme of this book has been the unswerving determination of the dominant political interests in the Western world, ever since the 1970s, to resist any change in the global economic order and structures of power that might weaken their own supremacy and disproportionate share of the world's wealth. Seen in the historical perspective of the last two centuries such obduracy might seem extreme. For since the advent of the French Revolution of 1789 and the Industrial Revolution which swept most of Europe in the early nineteenth century, there has been a general tendency for Western elites to make at least minimum concessions to those forces that might otherwise have unleashed more profound social and political upheaval. Thus over the succeeding 150 years traditional monarchical or aristocratic societies gave ground to 'bourgeois revolutions', and then to the progressive extension of voting rights to the whole population, while at the same time basic rights to health care, education and social protection – in the face of growing insecurity occasioned by the capitalist business cycle – were conceded.

Hence by the end of World War II the political establishment in the industrialised West had explicitly accepted that society was under an obligation to provide minimum standards of living and human dignity to all their people – or at least the vast majority. This seeming triumph of liberal/progressive values was reinforced by the unprecedented post-war economic boom lasting up to 1973. As noted in Chapter 1, however, this benign political consensus did not long survive the subsequent decline in global economic growth and prosperity. Yet the refusal of the ruling establishment to come to terms with what has been revealed since the 1980s as the chronic inability of latter-day capitalism to deliver a minimally acceptable degree of economic security to all but a small and dwindling minority remains total. This is evident from the growing degree of ideological uniformity being imposed on the body politic and on virtually all channels for expression of opinion – even in the face of further deterioration in the economic and financial outlook.

The continued dominance of such a uniformly illiberal and reactionary ideology is remarkable – even allowing for the impact of the Soviet Union's collapse in discrediting the whole idea of a collectivist alternative. Indeed it appears in striking contrast to the spirit of liberal pragmatism which, as suggested above, enabled the ruling elite to adjust, however painfully, to unavoidable change through the nineteenth century and much of the twentieth. It may be that the difference is to be explained by the virtual absence in the industrialised West of serious civil unrest – a more or less perpetual threat throughout the nineteenth century – during the long downward slide since the 1970s. This may in turn be attributable to the very success of the preceding post-war boom in bringing about economic and social transformation, such that the vast majority of the public came to believe in the system's capacity to deliver sustained improvements in their living standards. Hence despite the continuing decline in economic performance in the last quarter of the twentieth century – manifest in rising levels of unemployment and poverty as well as in the rising costs and deteriorating quality of many public services – the mass of the population has remained quiescent. The general perception that the economic situation and prospects remain tolerable has naturally been reinforced by official propaganda, which has also constantly held out the prospect of greater improvements in the longer term.

As has already been made clear, however, one crucial condition for continued acceptability of the status quo has been the avoidance until now of a deep and sustained fall in the value of financial securities to which the well-being of the vast majority of the population is now so directly linked. This is both because it would threaten a destruction of capital and livelihoods directly affecting hundreds of millions of people – on a scale at least as devastating as that caused by the financial meltdown of 1929–33 – and because it could finally bring the self-regulated profits system into terminal discredit.

For these very compelling reasons the ruling establishment has an obvious incentive to prevent or delay the onset of any such disaster. The numerous expedients and strategies adopted by the corporate sector to this end, usually with the full connivance of governments – culminating in the widespread resort to criminal abuses in the 1990s – have been elaborated in earlier chapters. Yet although the wave of scandals that have engulfed corporations in the USA and elsewhere since 2001 may seem a potentially mortal propaganda setback to the supporters of capitalism, it is perhaps difficult to claim (at the time of writing) that it is close to its terminal phase. The main reasons why the system's credibility has not yet been more widely called into question would appear to be:

- The impact of the collapse in financial markets and the associated acts of unparalleled fraud on the incomes and prospects of the mass of individual savers and investors – as well as corporate employees and pensioners – has yet to be fully felt.
- The ideological commitment of all mainstream political parties – as well as of opinion formers in the mass media and academia – to the maintenance of self-regulated capitalism remains outwardly unshaken.

For both these reasons it is still possible in 2004 for the ruling elite to exclude from the main channels of public debate any discussion of radical alternatives to the status quo which might call into question the fundamental assumptions of the self-regulated capitalist profits system. This striking rigidity – which is expressed in the almost total uniformity of support for neoliberal dogma – is imposed through the increasingly assertive dominance of corporate interests, with their vast financial resources, in the control of the political process and hence over the actions and pronouncements of public bodies (such as the World Bank, for example). In contrast to the reformist pragmatism which, as we have suggested, was typical of Western governments for most of the period since the Industrial Revolution, this inflexible stance of today's ruling establishment more closely resembles that of the old French aristocracy before the Revolution. For, just as in eighteenth-century France, today's elite perceive (with much justification) that any moves to water down their immense privileges would tend to lead to the effective demise of the structures – particularly those of the financial markets – on which their essentially parasitic power is based.[1]

In seeking to maintain the increasingly dysfunctional status quo, today's rulers have, as already noted, resorted to a number of distorting subterfuges designed to conceal the true nature of the gathering catastrophe from the general public – if not from themselves. Yet as these desperate expedients have inevitably failed to avert the onset of systemic collapse, those who would preserve the self-regulated profits system have found it necessary to resort to ever more outlandish denials of reality.

Falsifying the numbers

Just as it has become habitual among corporations and financial institutions to engage in blatant accounting fraud in order to paint a positive picture of their financial performance, governments have likewise resorted to falsifying the record of economic performance with a view to averting the onset of public pessimism – and a corresponding collapse in market confidence. Such distortions, which for obvious reasons are seldom exposed in the mass media, relate to the following areas in particular.

National income growth rates   As already noted, the fact that official statistics (published by the OECD and the IMF) show an unmistakable long-term downward trend in global economic growth since the 1970s is a reality that has long been studiously ignored in the public pronouncements of analysts and policymakers alike. In the United States, however, the government has gone even further in its desperation to hide the reality: by deliberately distorting the GDP statistics in order to exaggerate the true rate of economic growth. This has notably involved the use of the so-called 'hedonic deflator' to try and capture the supposed extra value to consumers of increases in the power and utility of computers by attributing to them a real value in the national accounts far greater than their actual market value. As a result this component of GDP 'measures dollars that nobody pays and nobody receives'.[2] Thus the surreal quality of this deception lies in the fact that it appears to be an attempt to convince investors who are bound to be true believers in the market economy – that is, that monetary transactions are the one true measure of value – that an essentially abstract definition of value can be regarded as a genuine indicator of profitability. It is analogous to telling a farmer whose wheat crop has been halved in value by a collapse in market prices that it is worth exactly the same per tonne as it was at last year's higher prices.

A further upward distortion in US GDP statistics has been achieved by counting the very substantial expenditure on computer software as capital investment (and thus an addition to GDP) rather than as a cost of production (resulting in a net reduction), as is done in all other countries. This is precisely analogous to the corporate accounting device of capitalising current costs – a practice that has been widely condemned in many of the recently exposed accounting frauds such as that of WorldCom.[3]

Inflation Just as growth statistics – at least in the United States – have been modified to reflect subjective official estimates of supposedly higher economic worth not reflected in market prices, so it has become the US practice to adjust official measures of price inflation downwards to allow for estimated improvements in the quality of consumer products. It is true that there is a theoretical case for such 'hedonic' adjustments, given the speed of technology-driven change in the design and quality of products such as audio equipment. However, it is clear that adjustments to allow for supposed improvements in value are bound to be subjective, while the fact that consumers may have no choice but to buy an improved and more expensive replacement for a less advanced product that has been withdrawn from the market (e.g. CDs rather than audio tapes) makes the use of such techniques as a basis for measuring changes in the cost of living seem obviously questionable.[4] Furthermore, suspicions as to the motives of the authorities are strengthened by the fact that the effect of such 'quality adjustments' to consumer price indices is invariably to keep the recorded rate of inflation below what it would otherwise have been. Given that such indices are used by governments (increasingly desperate to contain public spending levels) to determine the level of uprating of pensions and other benefits, it is all too easy to suspect the statistical authorities of having a conflict of interest. Furthermore there are strong grounds for believing that both the US and other governments[5] are relying greatly on such distortions of the official measure of inflation to try to perpetuate the post-bubble 'economic recovery' of 2003–04. For it is clear (as of April 2004) that continued belief in the sustainability of this supposed recovery depends on the assumption that the record low US short-term interest rates (1 per cent) in place since 2002 can be maintained and that this in turn depends on the perception that inflation is low. In the absence of such delusions interest rates would be forced higher and the financial weakness of many corporations fatally exposed.

Unemployment Perhaps because the maintenance of low levels of unemployment was long considered such a central goal of public policy in the industrialised countries, its measurement has become particularly prone to official distortion. This has been especially true in the period since the early 1970s when governments began to fail in their attempts to contain the steady rise in the numbers of jobless. By the end of that decade the recorded rate of unemployment in the OECD (industrialised) countries had doubled from 3 per cent of the labour force – roughly the level, deemed to be consistent with 'full employment', which had prevailed since 1950 – to 6 per cent. Although subsequently the ratio has undoubtedly risen much higher still in most of the countries concerned – to 12 to 15 per cent in some cases – this reality has seldom been reflected in the official statistics. Of the numerous subterfuges used to distort the true figures, the most significant is that of reclassifying the workless as disabled. This has affected a high proportion of the labour force in a number of countries – notably Britain, the Netherlands, Norway and the USA[6] – such that if those actually fit to work among the total receiving disability benefit were correctly classified they would probably add at least 3 per cent to the unemployment ratio. Hence it is likely that, as against an official figure of 6–7 per cent in the industrialised countries in 2003,[7] the true unemployment rate is at least 9–10 per cent according to the criteria of the early 1970s – a threefold rise compared with the earlier period. So far from recognising this reality, the establishment (led by none other than Kofi Annan, the UN secretary-general) sought in 2004 to propagate the myth that Western Europe faces a prospective chronic labour shortage, such that it now needs to import large numbers of migrant workers in order to sustain economic stability.[8]

Such systematic distortion of economic indicators by the authorities has an obvious two-fold purpose, namely

- to conceal from the general public the full extent of economic deterioration, and
- to promote a sense of optimism among investors so as to halt, if not reverse, the tide of selling that is engulfing the markets.

Undoubtedly the latter is the most crucial consideration in the eyes of both governments and the corporate establishment. For, with the fortunes of all major corporations and financial institutions – and through them the vast majority of the general public

– now irrevocably geared to the values of securities, there can be
no doubt of the dangers of further sustained market decline.

The response to the pensions crisis:
a study in fantasy

The immense social and political problems now looming as a
result of the sudden collapse of funded pension schemes in the
wake of the millennium market crash have been repeatedly referred to in earlier chapters. Because of its obviously intractable
nature, it is not surprising that the establishment has had particular problems in coming to terms with this phenomenon. What was
clearly inadmissible from the outset was any recognition that the
whole concept of funded pensions based on investment in inherently unstable financial assets was fundamentally flawed and ripe
for abolition. For this would have called into question the very
existence of vast swathes of the financial services sector, including
most of the fund management industry. Hence, instead of plac-
ing the blame on the obvious culprit, the official consensus has
been that it really lies with the retired population for rendering
funds insolvent by living longer than expected, while at the same
time their numbers are increasing relative to those of working
age people allegedly needed to support them – a phenomenon
referred to as the 'demographic time bomb'. This alibi has been
concocted despite the fact that the increasing longevity of the
population is merely the continuation of a trend which had been
observable throughout the twentieth century – and which had
not prevented many companies from suspending contributions to
pension funds during the stock market boom of the 1990s.[9]

From this warped diagnosis of the problem the consensus has
arrived at some quite amazingly irrational proposals for solving
it, including

- requiring fund members to work on beyond the present normal retirement age of 60 or 65 – perhaps until they are 70 or even 75 – before being entitled to draw their pension;
- encouraging people to have more children on the grounds that this will ultimately lead to a correction in the trend towards a supposedly excessive ratio of the retired population to the working population (thought to be especially necessary in those European countries where the total population is starting to decline).

The Alice in Wonderland perversity of these suggested solutions – which are supported by all mainstream political parties and virtually all organs of the press[10] – lies in the fact that they are made without any consideration of their likely impact on the balance of the labour market.[11] That serious policymakers and journalists can advance such ideas while ignoring the inconvenient fact that the countries concerned already have substantial levels of unemployment – which implementation of their proposals would potentially double – illustrates as graphically as anything the extent of the establishment's ideological bankruptcy.

Compulsive optimism in the markets

In the wake of the global stock market collapse that has occurred since March 2000 there has undoubtedly been widespread disillusion among the many individual investors who have lost substantial sums of money in the rout. Moreover, this feeling can only have been intensified by the subsequent exposure of extensive fraud and related abuses throughout the corporate and financial sectors. At the same time any investors who cared to try to determine the advisability of buying back into the market based on a hard-headed assessment of fundamental value would have recognised that share prices have remained just as overvalued as they were on the eve of the crash in 1999 (see Chapter 2) – as earnings had fallen almost as fast as prices. Adding yet another reason for pessimism, it was not hard to see that virtually every major sector of the global economy was weighed down with excess capacity. Hence not only was there little prospect of renewed opportunities for real investment (as opposed to speculation) but competitive pressures would severely restrict the scope for raising prices. Finally, it might have been supposed that the ability of corporations and investment analysts to overstate profit levels – with a view to inflating share values unduly – would be somewhat inhibited in the post-Enron climate of regulatory tightening.

It thus seems remarkable that in 2003, against such an overwhelmingly discouraging background, a solid body of opinion within the financial community succeeded in promoting the view that the time was ripe for a sustained recovery in the stock market. The result was a rally that saw by the end of 2003 the main US stock exchange indices rise by 30 per cent or more in nine months, with corresponding gains in most other markets around the world.

Superficially, this rally may appear to have had some justification in that there had been a degree of recovery in reported profits from the depressed levels of 2001–02. However, it is clear that in most cases this improvement has been largely the result of the retrenchment and cost cutting which are typical of corporate response to a downswing in the business cycle but for which there is likely to be limited scope in subsequent years. Meanwhile there has predictably been no sign of a significant upturn in corporate revenues – such as would be needed to underpin a sustained market recovery – despite numerous reported sightings of a revival in demand in one part or another of the global economy.

In reality it must be concluded that there was no objective justification at all for such a sharp and sustained rally. This judgement is reinforced by the fact that it was ostensibly sparked off by the start of the US/British invasion of Iraq in March 2003 – an event which seemed to give little cause for economic optimism at the time and which has subsequently given quite the opposite. Hence the action of investors in pushing up share prices so soon after the millennium crash can be seen as a return to the 'irrational exuberance'[12] that drove the market bubble of the 1990s. This was even extended to renewed enthusiasm for many of the dotcom stocks so widely thought to have been completely discredited by their collapse three years earlier. Thus Amazon.com, a star of the earlier dotcom mania, saw its share price rise fivefold between the start of 2002 and December 2003 – even though it had never made a genuine profit.

Another sign of nostalgia for the discredited investment fantasies of the 1990s has been the renewed enthusiasm from 2003 for the stock markets of East Asia – with the glaring exception of Japan. This facile euphoria has been based on a refusal to recognise the obvious signs that

- The revival of growth in countries like South Korea and Thailand in 2002–03 was based on an artificial and unsustainable pumping up of domestic demand which is bound to end in a new round of massive bad debts;
- The current largely export-oriented boom in China mirrors that of the early 1990s in the Asian 'tiger' economies – and is thus equally bound to end in tears. For like the earlier bubble it is based mainly on a one-off transfer of productive capacity from already industrialised countries – in this case principally the USA rather than Japan – to take advantage of cheap labour. Equally, it has been underpinned by enormous,

market-distorting capital subsidies provided by the essentially insolvent state banks.[13]

Another surreal symptom of what has been called the 'echo bubble' of 2003 is the sudden revival in the last quarter of the year of merger and acquisition (M&A) activity in both the USA and Europe. This is particularly remarkable in view of the well publicised M&A disasters exposed by the millennium crash (see Chapter 3) and of the fact that it has consequently become the conventional wisdom that mergers almost invariably result in the destruction of shareholder value – at least for the acquiring company.[14] In fact a number of large shareholders have voiced protests against this remarkable apparent triumph of hope over experience.[15] However, given the inevitable flaws in the capitalist model of corporate governance referred to in the last chapter, it is scarcely surprising to find that the large shareholders' ability to prevent such perverse transactions – against the will of the combined vested interests of management and investment bankers – is no greater than before.

Such apparently irrational behaviour by investor organisations calls for some explanation. In fact, it may well be linked to their broader collective concern to help boost optimism about market prospects. For given the strong vested interest of the major investment institutions in averting total market meltdown, it is not unreasonable to suppose that there may have been some concerted action between them in order to try to move the market decisively upwards. It is obvious that such attempts at market rigging are only likely to be undertaken by relatively large institutions, which (a) can combine to achieve sufficient critical mass to move the market and (b) are risking other people's money rather than their own in what they must clearly see as very risky speculation. Perhaps more decisively, there are clear indications that the US authorities have sent tacit signals that they will lend their support to efforts to reinflate the market both by ensuring that more or less limitless credit is available and even by engaging in discreet purchases of stocks themselves. In fact such mechanisms for providing official support to the market, which have long been openly applied in Japan and other Asian markets, have been in place in the United States since the market 'crash' of 1987. For understandable reasons, however, the activities of the President's Working Group on Financial Markets – popularly known as the 'Plunge Protection Team' – have been little publicised. In fact it may well be the case that its importance lies less in its actual purchasing interventions in the market than in the psychological impact of its very existence and the belief thereby instilled in the markets that the authorities stand ready to intervene in their support when necessary.

Whatever the precise nature and effect of such interventions, there can be no doubt as to the purpose behind them. For it is evident that such a rise in the value of securities is seen as vital to the commercial survival of large numbers of financial and non-financial corporations threatened with insolvency by the continuing steep decline in securities markets – not to mention the possibility of total systemic meltdown. Yet it must surely be understood by anyone who has not completely lost touch with reality that such ploys, added to subsidised credit and other life-support mechanisms, only serve to perpetuate the overcapacity that is strangling the economy and pushing everyone closer to bankruptcy – as demonstrated by recent Japanese experience (see Chapter 1).

An admission of defeat?

None but the most bigoted supporters of contemporary capital-ism, it might be thought, could fail to see that such actions as

official intervention in the market to support share prices represent the ultimate betrayal of the values on which capitalism is
supposed to be based. Yet such has been the effect of decades
of moral hazard that we should perhaps hardly be surprised if
such actions are accepted as normal by many people who should
know better. An indication of such attitudes is provided by a proposal, evidently made in all seriousness by a respected think-tank,
that the US government should extend its effective guarantee of
bank deposits and pension funds to investments by individuals
in financial securities.[16] Strikingly, when the author asked those
responsible for this suggestion whether it would not undermine
the rationale of the risk/reward principle (central to the justification for market capitalism) he received the reply that 'while the
risk/reward principle may be a good one in the abstract it mostly
doesn't exist in the US financial system'. While such candour is
in refreshing contrast to the pronouncements of the chairman
of the Federal Reserve Board and other government officials, it
starkly demonstrates the extent of latter-day capitalism's detach-
ment from its ideological roots and the dwindling acceptance of
the traditional notion of market discipline. More significantly, it
is reasonable to see it as an effective admission that the capitalist
profits system has finally been exposed as too dysfunctional to be
tolerable in a civilised society.

Just as fatally, however, it should be obvious to those who
advocate such institutionalized market distortion that it will inevitably tend to deter private investment in new enterprises and
undermine the viability of existing ones. This is well illustrated
by the flood of speculative investment funds that has poured into
online retailing businesses – which have mostly never made any
genuine profits – as an expression of 'dotcom mania' (still not
dead even following the bursting of the original bubble, as noted
above). For by making available what amounts to free capital to

these new enterprises the distorted financial markets are also serving to damage existing conventional retailers by effectively subsidising competition. Hence such processes have merely added to the chronic artificial oversupply of markets and are thus serving to perpetuate low profitability.

The triumph of mendacity over experience

Such negations of the fundamental principles of market capitalism in the actions of the global establishment have not gone totally unremarked or unopposed – even among supporters of the system. Yet most mainstream dissenters clamour for a restoration of financial orthodoxy and traditional market discipline, pointing out (correctly) that the efforts of the authorities, orchestrated by the chairman of the US Federal Reserve, to avert a major market correction by creating one credit-driven financial bubble after another, will only make the ultimate meltdown even more catastrophic than it would have been anyway.[17] Supporters of this approach often identify themselves with the so-called Austrian school of economists, prominent before World War II, who tended to regard the downward shifts of the business cycle as an acceptable price to pay for the benefits of capitalism – and even as a positive source of 'creative destruction'.[18] Yet for all the validity of their critique these commentators evidently fail to grasp that, whatever action is now taken within a traditional market framework, it is too late to prevent an economic cataclysm so severe as to threaten the ultimate survival of the capitalist profits system itself.

It is ironic that those who actually hold the reins of power have, since the rise of neoliberal ideology in the 1980s, acquired the image of extreme advocates of laissez-faire, insisting as they do on the importance of maximum deregulation of markets. The fact that they have in reality offset the impact of such superficial liberalisation with ever greater degrees of market manipulation and distortion – as illustrated throughout this book – is a measure of their complete abandonment of principle in the face of inescapable cyclical disaster. This strategy, as already noted, can be seen as essentially Keynesian to the extent that it rests primarily on providing state support for private enterprise in the increasingly forlorn hope that this will eventually bring about a sustained upturn in growth.

Indeed, as prospects of a genuine recovery have become ever more elusive, there have since the 1990s been increasing signs of reversion to crudely Keynesian macroeconomic policies – of a kind that had supposedly been rejected at the end of the 1970s in favour of 'monetarism'. This is reflected in

- The extreme monetary laxity of the US authorities, particularly since the stock markets began their steep fall in 2000. This has facilitated the continued inflation of an enormous credit bubble with a view both to maintaining the growth of consumer demand and enabling financially weakened businesses to avoid insolvency by refinancing their debts. If the European Central Bank has not followed this example this is perhaps only because it feels compelled zealously to guard the new single currency – launched in 1999 – against any possible risk of inflation.
- Moves to relax budgetary discipline. Following two decades in which the industrialised countries' chronic fiscal deficits had led to a doubling in their ratio of public indebtedness to GDP,[19] by the late 1990s this explosion had been brought under control – except in Japan, where continuing stagnation led the government repeatedly to boost public spending in vain efforts

to 'kick-start' the economy. With the bursting of the stock market bubble in 2000, however, the USA suddenly saw its newly achieved federal fiscal surplus start to evaporate, while at state level budget deficits reached their highest level for fifty years by 2002.[20] The response of the Bush administration – a large tax cut targeted mainly at higher earners – clearly rests on the hope that deficit financing will succeed in reviving sustained growth in the USA where it has thus far failed in Japan. Likewise in the Eurozone, member states led by France and Germany were by late 2003 in open revolt against the ironically named Stability and Growth Pact, designed to contain fiscal deficits in the interests of enhancing the credibility of the new single currency.

This tendency to resort once again to the failed strategies of the past only serves to highlight the essential vacuity of official strategy. It also emphasises the central flaw in the thinking of policymakers: their compulsive denial of the abiding constraints to growth. The net result is that a return to large budget deficits in the industrialised countries – with a consequently renewed explosive rise in public debt – is now unavoidable, with potentially alarming implications for both inflation and currency stability.

It is impossible to believe that key figures in the ruling establishment are unaware of the dangerously unbalanced state of the global economy and of the certainty that the longer they promote further bubble excesses and moral hazard the more catastrophic the eventual meltdown is bound to be. Indeed the fact that Chairman Greenspan of the US Federal Reserve warned of the overvaluation of the stock market in 1996, only to give his blessing three years later to stock prices which had doubled again in the meantime, most obviously demonstrates his understanding of the dangers. Just as obviously, however, it shows his growing awareness of his inability to bring the situation under control without precipitating precisely the market meltdown he had earlier sought to avert. More cynically, along with most other corporate and financial leaders, he may have concluded that, given the inevitability of the ultimate market bust, the most sensible course for those with the wealth, knowledge and power to exploit the situation is to make one last killing before the ultimate deluge.

For any who may have doubted the capacity of the ruling elite to act so irresponsibly, the easy complicity of both the magnates of Wall Street and successive administrations in Washington in the breathtaking crimes of Enron and WorldCom has probably dispelled any illusions. Indeed the insouciance with which the Bush administration is prepared, in the midst of such a huge financial crisis, both to implement a massive tax cut (benefiting mainly the rich) and launch a costly and unprovoked war in Iraq suggests a regime utterly heedless of public welfare – and willing to do anything either to gain a short-term reprieve or to try and distract public attention from what is happening. As such it calls to mind the increasingly criminal behaviour of the Soviet hierarchy in its terminal phase – and the shamelessly corrupt conduct of its post-Soviet successors (notably under Boris Yeltsin) – in looting the assets of an already bankrupt economy and thus condemning most of the people to destitution.

Perhaps the most chilling reflection evoked by these manifestations of degeneracy is that a force indistinguishable from organised crime may have gained effective control of the world's most powerful governments – as has manifestly happened in the case of some major corporations.[21] If indeed this has happened – or is in the process of happening – it should perhaps be seen as merely the inevitable outcome of the mixed economy regime which has institutionalised conflict of interest and moral hazard by allowing private profit-making corporations to identify their interests with those of the public. For ultimately, as is well known, any such easy opportunity for making corrupt profits is bound to attract criminal interests. The most spectacular and best-documented instance of this was the scandal of the newly deregulated US Savings and Loan industry of the 1980s. This involved an unprecedented orgy of fraudulent lending and bankruptcy, in which the family of President George H.W. Bush was significantly implicated, and which culminated in a bail-out instigated by the same president in 1989, ultimately costing the US taxpayer some $1.4 trillion.[22] Further evidence for believing that criminal infiltration of the US government may indeed be a reality is provided by the fact that in 2001 the second Bush administration initially sought to limit international restraints on money laundering, a mechanism which the Mafia is well known to employ in covering its tracks.[23] Such actions are also consistent with the failure of US and other Western leaders to act vigorously to bring the perpetrators of crimes such as those at Enron to justice. Likewise it is hard to explain official unconcern at the threat to economic and social stability posed by maintaining such a ruinous policy as the free flow of international capital except in terms of high-level connivance at fraud. For the continued insistence of Washington on imposing this facility on weak economies where it can only perpetuate ruin – against the soundly based advice of its own experts – can only be understood as an effective conspiracy of financial concerns willing and able to pursue their own interests at the expense of those of the public (see Chapter 4).

The idea that the legally constituted governments of the United States, Britain or other Western countries might be thus infiltrated by organised crime naturally tends to be rejected by most of their citizens as inconceivable. Such understandable reflex opinions are of course a source of great strength for the corrupt rulers who abuse their trust. It remains to be seen how long the public's complacency can withstand the torrent of revelations of malfeasance revealed by the current systemic crisis. Equally it may be wondered how long it will be before the irresponsible and parasitic forces that dominate the system effectively kill the body on which they feed.[24] That such a danger exists may be taken as a sign that, even if we can conclude that the world is in thrall to a conspiracy, it is one that is definitely out of control.

7

Beyond the Cataclysm

The preceding chapters have described both the manifest break-down in the functioning of the global economic order based on the capitalist profits system and the intransigent resistance by the ruling establishment to any radical reforms such as would be needed to render it less destructive – or even to recognising the reality of the problem. As noted, this resistance is quite under-standable in the light of historical precedents – which suggest that parasitic elites always tend to fight to the bitter end to pre-serve their unjustifiable privileges.

It is, of course, true that at the dawn of the twenty-first century we live in a world where institutionalised privilege is supposed to have been subordinated to the popular will, thanks to the spread of universal suffrage and of the idea of universal human rights. Hence in a theoretically more democratic climate than prevailed in eighteenth-century France or in Russia before the collapse of tsarism – or indeed that of Communism – it might be expected that Western society would have developed the capacity to adjust to inevitable change without the need for violent revolution. If in fact there is reason to doubt that modern political institutions can prove any more flexible than those of the authoritarian past, it would seem to be ascribable to (a) the enormous power that moneyed interests have acquired to influence the 'democratic' process – to the point of effectively buying whole political parties or governments, and (b) the related capacity (much aided by modern technology) to indoctrinate the public with irrational ideology through the mass media (inevitably dominated by the same monied interests).

Given the seemingly monolithic stance of mainstream political leaders and analysts against any suggestion of a need for radical change from the status quo, it is difficult to foresee quite what precise event in the unfolding breakdown might precipitate a decisive breach in the defensive wall. It is certainly possible to argue that the motivation behind the spreading global threat of terrorism is linked to the deepening frustration felt by so many in the Third World at the failure of Western-imposed globalisation to contain or reduce poverty. Strikingly, just such a connection has been made by none other than the president of the World Bank, James Wolfensohn[1] – even though most Western political leaders still shrink from doing so. It is easier to believe that a serious political explosion in the industrialised world (the epicentre of global power) could be sparked by some economic disaster that affects the people of those countries more directly. This might perhaps be either a general collapse in the value of the world's major currencies – possibly linked to the failure of financial institutions, which the authorities were no longer able to bail out – or that depositors and savers of failed institutions might combine with cheated pensioners, employees and shareholders of other bankrupt corporations in widespread civil disorder. It is far from obvious, however, that in such circumstances governments will have any contingency plans capable of bringing the situation under control – other than perhaps some strategy of more or less crude repression.

Moreover, bearing in mind the sustained brainwashing that has been applied across the whole of society (through the education system as well as the media), it is difficult to imagine precisely what alternative agendas might be articulated by any emerging forces of opposition once these were enabled to crystallise. Yet as suggested in earlier chapters, one theme that seems certain to become increasingly dominant is the demand to bring the corporate sector (whether nominally private or public) under a form of regulation that renders it more genuinely accountable to society as a whole. Indeed if the steadily rising public concern over this issue in the wake of recent disasters is not very soon allayed by a totally improbable recovery in economic and corporate performance, it is hard to imagine that a much more far-reaching reform of the existing order will not be demanded.

It seems likely that two basic premisses of any agenda for fundamental change that might emerge would be:

- The model of self-regulated, profit-maximising capitalism is no longer compatible with the priorities of modern democracies.
- The policy aim of indiscriminately maximising the rate of economic growth, based on a competitive struggle for markets, must be abandoned in favour of increasing emphasis on redistribution of income and wealth based on principles of equity and cooperation.

The linkage between these two essential themes of a more sustainable order should be clear. For in a modern democracy the continued justification for the capitalist profits system must rest on its ability to deliver growth which can be sustained at a level high enough to ensure both (a) an adequate return on capital for investors and (b) adequate and stable living standards for the vast majority of the population. Yet as demonstrated in earlier chapters, it is now irrefutably plain that there are limits to expanding the output of goods and services perpetually, in line with the continuing exponential rise in global productive capacity (because of short-term limits to demand growth, if not environmental constraints as well). For this reason the traditional business cycle of boom and bust is today as much part of capitalist reality as ever – while the threat it poses is compounded by the impact of technological change both on the demand for capital and in altering its very nature (see Chapter 3). Furthermore, if it is accepted that the scope for expanding output must – over a given time period – be restricted to less than the potential productive capacity of the available labour force, it must also follow that there needs to be a greater degree of equality in the distribution of income than if society were to continue harbouring the illusion that high growth was infinitely sustainable.

A new dispensation for enterprise

Given the inescapable recognition of such reality, it would be impossible to avoid accepting, in place of the traditional deregulated model of economy, a far more rigorous structure of corporate and political accountability, enshrining the principles that

- Any enterprise (whether private or publicly owned) will only be allowed to trade within a given market (national or regional) if it is in compliance with a common regulatory regime reflecting public priorities (e.g. relating to labour standards, taxation or the environment). This would be essential to avoid any recurrence of the competitive 'race to the bottom' which so disfigures latter-day global capitalism.

- Any enterprise receiving special privileges or protection (including limited liability) from the state must accept public representation on its governing body, with ultimate right of official veto (through democratically accountable bodies at regional, national or local level) over key policy decisions – i.e. including such matters as investment and employment.
- Reform of the democratic process (including restraints on control of the mass media) must ensure that it is no longer open to undue influence (through financial contributions to politicians or parties) by business or other sectional interests.

From the acceptance of such principles it would tend to follow that:

- Profit maximisation (the primary concern of shareholders, in whose interests corporations must be run under existing company law) would be downgraded as an objective.
- In consequence of this downgrading the role of private capital in enterprise investment would be progressively reduced, as shareholders perceived the prospective return on capital to be too great to compensate them for the risk of loss – except in relatively small enterprises where ownership and control could be combined and dependence on official protection avoided.
- Growth would cease to be a priority of either corporate or government policy – except to the extent it was seen as necessary to raise the level of economic activity and employment in relatively impoverished regions or countries.

In the absence of the stimulus of profit maximisation, other criteria would have to be applied to provide a spur to optimum efficiency. These would have to include measurable performance targets linked to incentives – the determination and application of which would need to be subjected to transparent scrutiny and audit. At the same time the allocation of resources (which will be increasingly under the implicit guarantee of the state) for investment in and support of enterprise and employment will have to be subject to transparent and equitable criteria. For even in the absence of a strong capitalist profit motive there will still be pressure, under conditions of restricted growth in demand, for enterprises to take market share away from each other. Hence regulatory vigilance to prevent unfair competition – whether through predatory pricing or disguised subsidies (including those aimed at protecting the inefficient) – will be essential. More broadly, however, as suggested above, it would be desirable to place greater emphasis on cooperation rather than competition in a world where the damaging consequences of the latter are increasingly more apparent than its benefits.[2]

Reordering economic priorities

The most liberating feature of such a new dispensation – in which society would no longer be a slave to the ideology of maximisation of growth and corporate profits – is that a significant proportion of economic value-added (i.e. GDP) could be diverted from satisfying shareholders and speculators to serve other priorities. The crucial point about the determination of such priorities is that it would be made on the basis of conscious political choices rather than in accordance with either the blind dictates of market forces or the self-serving agenda of a few unaccountable corporate executives.

What is less clear is precisely what proportion of GDP would be released for such purposes as a result of the virtual phasing out of profit appropriation by enterprises, since reliable and comparable estimates of the share of corporate profits are hard to come by for most countries. Based on official national accounts statistics for the United States and Britain from 1990 to 2000 it would appear that the share of corporate profits after tax in GDP averaged somewhere in the range of 8–12 per cent. If, however, the vast bulk of value-added absorbed by debt service and payments made to other more or less parasitic financial institutions is also taken into account (as it should be), it is reasonable to assume that 15 per cent or more of GDP would become available for more economically and socially valuable uses.[3] The same is true of the ever more inflated salaries, bonuses, share options and fees sliced off value-added by corporate chief executives, directors, investment bankers, lawyers, management consultants and assorted hangers-on.

Likewise there must follow a reversal of the liberalising/privatising trend of the 1980s and 1990s which has resulted in both a sucking of value-added from the traditional public sector and (as is now progressively dawning on public opinion) an inevitable loss in cost-effectiveness of the public services involved. Even more inevitably there will need to be a complete abandonment of the totally misconceived and now bankrupt model of funded pensions linked to securities markets in favour of pay-as-you-go state pension schemes not dependent on uncertain asset values. All these unavoidable implications of the dethroning of the profit motive are obviously quite fatal to the presently dominant vested interests who control big business and (through the latter) the political process. Indeed it is precisely this prospect that concentrates the mind of the princes of finance capital in Wall Street and the City of London – whose very *raison d'être* is fund management and speculative dealing in corporate assets – on the desperate struggle to avoid their fate.

It is, of course, true that substituting management structures based on democratic accountability for the destructive chaos of the existing regime will make the decision-making process much more complex and time-consuming than at present. There is likewise no guarantee that even the theoretically most representative democratic structures will arrive at decisions on resource allocation or legislation that will either be wise or command durable support. Yet it should at least no longer be possible to try to impose such decisions on the simplistic grounds that they are required by pitiless and supposedly irresistible market forces – which is really no different from primitive notions that 'the gods demand sacrifices' or Adam Smith's purely metaphysical concept of the Hidden Hand.

It may seem self-evident that the highest priority for the alternative use of presently misallocated resources and unjustly expropriated value-added would be a fundamental redistribution of income based on principles of equity and sustainability. The crucial importance of such a radical change of direction would be all the greater not only because of the vast and unjustified inequalities in remuneration that have arisen between top executives and the mass of employees. An equally vital consideration would be the need to find ways of providing adequate incomes for the vast numbers of people who are presently either unemployed (but have been largely airbrushed out of the jobless statistics) or else are engaged in activities not recognised as part of the capitalist economy. The latter category most obviously includes those unpaid or underpaid 'carers' who have been called on increasingly to bear the burden of looking after the elderly and infirm which capitalist society manifestly cannot afford. A drastic reform of income distribution along these lines would permit the restoration of the interconnected issues of income, employment and social welfare to the central position on the political agenda that they once enjoyed – after years in which their neglect has inflicted massive damage on the social and economic fabric. At the same time the removal of profit-maximising considerations from the equation would make it possible to take account of the effects of technological change – and the huge rise in the productivity of labour relative to the demand for it – in determining the allocation of employment and incomes. While it cannot be claimed that it would be easy to devise non-market mechanisms for determining incomes, it would be equally impossible to shirk the task – in a world where traditional notions of full employment have been rendered obsolete – if ever more millions are to avoid economic marginalisation.

Averting total collapse

The present seeming paralysis of the global establishment in face of the manifest economic and social disintegration that is now unfolding is obviously deeply depressing for any who would seek to move the world towards the kind of radically new economic model briefly outlined above. For even if, for reasons already given, such intransigence is understandable, it raises the possibility – indeed the probability – that social and political tensions will build to an explosive level in response to deepening economic failure. At the same time the danger of systemic financial collapse – involving the outright insolvency of major financial and non-financial companies – grows more imminent by the year.

Since the ruling elite have largely managed to stifle any discussion of meaningful change to the status quo – and may well have thereby convinced themselves that it is not required – it must be doubted whether they have even prepared any contingency plans for dealing with such a breakdown. Indeed, this seems all the more likely in view of the signs of an increasingly cavalier attitude to the principles of sound financial management now pervading the Western establishment (see Chapter 6). Yet in the event of a major financial catastrophe – entailing mass corporate bankruptcy, a huge rise in unemployment and the consequent imminent destitution of millions (including pensioners) – drastic emergency measures would need to be implemented in order to contain the situation pending the implementation of longer-term structural change. While it is hard to visualise the precise circumstances that might arise, it seems probable that the immediate response would have to be a form of 'collective receivership' undertaken by national governments, including:

- mass state appropriation (at least on a temporary basis) of insolvent companies and financial institutions so as to permit normal trading to continue as far as possible;
- general suspension of debts pending their resolution on a transparent and equitable basis (case by case) over years;
- suspension of free cross-border movement of capital (involving the application of tight foreign-exchange controls);
- increased flows of supervised direct aid to prop up already insolvent Third World countries on an interim basis (this would in fact be an extension, on a vastly bigger scale, of the current covert and ad hoc strategy of Western governments of providing budgetary support to countries in Africa and elsewhere);
- tight supervision and control of international trade flows so as to minimise disruption of activity and avert the danger of open trade warfare.

In view of the sudden increase in public expenditure thus necessitated, combined with the effect of a sharp drop in public revenues, the solvency of the state itself might be called in question in most if not all industrialised countries – particularly in view of their existing high levels of indebtedness. It would thus be necessary to contemplate drastic measures to avoid total currency collapse. This would probably involve, in addition to the above measures, generalised official control of prices and incomes and direction of credit on an emergency basis.

Resistance and repression

In a world where, for all the palpable signs of unfolding economic disaster, established political parties remain monolithically wedded to maintaining the existing order largely intact, it may seem quixotic to advance proposals for radical change, even in the most general terms. For with the continuing abdication of responsibility by mainstream parties of the Left and their supposed allies in the trade unions (all of whom appear to have been effectively bought or brainwashed by the battalions of big business) there remains little scope for the advocacy of new ideas in places where they can have a chance of being discussed by more than isolated factions. To the extent that this enormous vacuum of leadership is being filled at all it is being done by the mushrooming anti-capitalist, anti-globalisation movements that have emerged since the late 1990s.[4]

Yet, as both supporters and critics of these movements have pointed out, they have a much clearer idea of what they are against than of what they are for, a weakness which is both cause and effect of their lack of leadership or structural coherence. Precisely how, if at all, such tendencies can coalesce or contribute to the creation of effective instruments of political change is by no means clear at the time of writing. However, even if their fragmentation and deficiency both in resources and in critical mass of popular support mean that they will remain a marginal political force for the time being, their importance as a focus of protest seems bound to increase as material conditions get worse for a growing majority of the population.

Meanwhile the ruling elite is plainly aware that its neoliberal ideology is losing credibility among the mass of voters in the Western industrialised world who constitute the essential core of their global power base. Equally, while they continue to exploit their dominance of the media to prevent the expression of any meaningful dissent, they undoubtedly recognise the need to do something to distract the public from the increasingly obvious 'disconnect' between rhetoric and reality. This seems to be the most plausible explanation for the otherwise wholly futile 'war on terror' launched by the USA in the wake of the horrific atrocities in New York and Washington of September 2001, as well as the illegal and superficially pointless US–British attack on Iraq in 2003. Whatever the true reasons for these ruinous campaigns, accompanied by undisguised assaults on human rights in the name of anti-terrorist security and a general tendency to intensify the climate of fear, it would be entirely consistent with past experience if they were shown to be intended primarily as a diversion from the economic failings and crimes of the Western leadership. For there can be no doubt that many threatened regimes in the past – notably in Europe and Japan of the 1930s – have sought to distract from economic collapse by appealing to extreme nationalist bigotry, if not outright fascism.

The upsurge of worldwide dissent in response to evident systemic failure, which has been most powerfully voiced in the developed world, has been matched by another scarcely containable threat to the existing global order, namely the spreading erosion of civil authority in the Third World – and even in many parts of the former Soviet bloc. The resulting social and economic chaos has led to such manifestations as

- the progressive disintegration of society and the economy in more and more 'developing' countries (of which Colombia,

Liberia, Somalia, the Democratic Republic of the Congo, Afghanistan and Nepal are only the most conspicuous examples) – to the point where there is either no government or its writ has ceased to run in large parts of the country;

- an explosion in the numbers of political refugees and economic migrants fleeing their own countries for the developed regions of Western Europe, North America and Australasia in search of a more secure existence;
- a proliferation of illicit trade and terrorist activity, both stimulated and facilitated by the spread of lawlessness and economic anarchy to an increasing portion of the world's territory.

For much of the 1990s the response of the Western establishment to these mounting symptoms of global disorder was one of silent impotence or studied ignorance – particularly in relation to Africa. For long the US leadership sought to convince itself that this was not a continent of vital interest to it – particularly following its humiliatingly abortive attempt to intervene in Somalia in 1992–93 – and that it could effectively isolate itself from the anarchy spreading across the whole continent. Such delusions were dispelled by the attacks on its embassies in East Africa in 1998, while at the same time terrorist attacks in other continents posed a growing challenge to Western complacency long before September 2001.

It is clear that the rising tide of worldwide resistance arises from grievances that are not exclusively linked to material deprivation, the most obvious of which is the increasingly bitter conflict in Palestine. It is nevertheless striking that the Western political mainstream remains adamant in its refusal to re-examine any of the fundamental elements of a global economic order which has so conspicuously failed to prevent massive material deprivation and social breakdown across most of the world.[5] But even though, as we have suggested, this obdurate reaction of the ruling elite to such manifest failure is understandable in historical terms, those charged with formulating official policy responses to the mounting disorder can no longer conceal the essential bankruptcy of their position.

An age of unreason?

For even if it is now accepted by Western leaders that the problem of deepening global chaos cannot be ignored any longer, their response appears to be totally incoherent and unrealistic – to the extent that it is possible to identify any strategy at all. At times indeed it seems to amount to retreating into a time-warp in which modern political and economic realities – or indeed any recognition of historical developments of the last two hundred years – are scarcely allowed to obtrude. In this fantasy world the current problem of global disorder is defined as one of 'failed states', which are seen as having proved incapable of establishing or maintaining the minimum elements of order and stability compatible with the needs of a modern society. The solution, it is now being suggested, must be to reimpose some form of imperial hegemony of the stronger nation-states over the weak or collapsed ones. What is most astonishing about such proposals – which are not yet official policy but have been adumbrated in writings of senior US and British foreign-policy experts much publicised in the press[6] – is not just that they constitute a rejection of the fundamental principles of modern international relations, but that they hark back to the European age of absolutism of the seventeenth century. As such the analysis behind this vision

- foresees a return to an order such as would have been approved of by Machiavelli or Hobbes, in which power and authority belong to those possessing the greatest military strength and lesser mortals must submit to the dictates of the strong;

- disregards totally the evolution of Western society since the eighteenth-century Enlightenment towards acceptance of ideas such as universal human rights, democracy and the rule of law (on which the United Nations Charter and the present world order are supposed to be based);
- ignores completely the economic imperatives of the global capitalist order (itself a product of the Enlightenment) and the issues raised by its present intractable problems.

The enormity of such reactionary imaginings might suggest they are not even worthy of mention. However, their significance lies in the fact that

- they emanate from sources close to the very centre of Anglo-American political authority;
- their hopelessly distorted and intellectually disreputable analysis is carefully dressed in the garb of supposedly respectable academic scholarship;
- their thesis is startlingly consistent with the present US strategy of nakedly seeking to subvert the whole idea of the international rule of law (by, for instance, undermining the authority of the UN Security Council in relation to international security and by seeking to strangle the International Criminal Court at birth).

It may thus not be too fanciful to suppose that the ruling oligarchy in Washington is trying to create a climate in which military conflict of one kind or another is considered a normal state of affairs and where consequently normal legal processes and human rights can be suspended in a more or less permanent state of emergency. Yet if this is indeed the intention it would suggest that those concerned have consciously embarked on what they must know to be a very high-risk strategy. For it is hard to believe they have failed to take account of the damaging impact such conditions could have on an already poor climate for investment and economic growth – one symptom of which is the depressed state of the airline and travel industry, particularly since September 2001. Alternatively they may have calculated, quite realistically, that there is now no escape from a catastrophic financial and economic slump, and that their only path to political survival lies in creating distractions and fabricating scapegoats.

Such a profoundly irresponsible attitude would be all too consistent with the spirit of grasping criminality which, as demonstrated by the countless scandals that have been exposed since the start of the crash, now pervades the Western establishment. Indeed, as heavily indebted governments are induced to offer more and more handouts to private enterprise (such as tax cuts or bail-outs of privatised utilities), while also finding more taxpayers' money to pay for unnecessary wars, a pattern reminiscent of the declining Soviet Union seems to emerge. Thus the reckless attitude to public finances, the looting of state assets, the refusal to address hopeless economic imbalances and mounting deprivation – all to the accompaniment of systematic misinformation – are indicative of a leadership which has effectively abandoned its stewardship of the public's welfare, with each of its members now scrambling for the exits with as much booty as he or she can carry. Likewise the involvement of organised crime is another feature characteristic of the collapsing Soviet Union.

It must obviously be hoped that such a depressing interpretation of the deepening chaos now manifest in the conduct of international affairs in general – and in the management of the global economy in particular – proves to be too pessimistic. Yet to the extent that no alternative leadership is soon enabled to emerge, offering some radical way out of the dead end at which the capitalist profits system has now arrived, such a nightmarish outcome must be considered both plausible and imminent. In that event the prospect of moving towards a more sustainable model – such as that briefly outlined above – will clearly become remote. Instead the world may all too easily continue its slide into an ever greater anarchy, from which it would be hard to foresee early deliverance. Such an eventuality will sorely test the resilience of human civilisation and the faith of those who would believe in its abiding capacity to progress.

Notes

Introduction

1. See Murray Weidenbaum (former chief economic adviser to President Reagan), 'Little Profit in Attack on Capitalism', *Christian Science Monitor*, 3 September 1998.
2. See *World Development Report 1987*, World Bank, Washington DC, 1987; Ha-Joon Chang, 'The Political Economy of Industrial Policy in Korea', *Cambridge Journal of Economics* 17, 1993, pp. 131–57.
3. World Bank, *China – Basic Health Services Project Appraisal 1998*, World Bank, Washington DC, 1998.
4. Harry Shutt, *The Trouble with Capitalism: An Enquiry into the Causes of Global Economic Failure*, Zed Books, London, 1998.

Chapter 1

1. As notably set out in the British government's famous White Paper on Employment Policy, Cmnd 6527, HMSO 1944.
2. In fact the pattern varied considerably, with often close (if still informal) involvement of government in determining the policy of key private corporations in parts of continental Europe and still

stronger influence in Japan. In all cases, however, such 'corporatist' relationships remained far from transparent and thus barely subject to genuine public accountability.

3. See Shutt, *The Trouble with Capitalism*, p. 37.

4. The author is indebted to a reviewer of *The Trouble with Capitalism* for pointing out his failure to make this connection clearly enough in the earlier work – see Edward Chase in *Challenge: The Magazine of Economic Affairs*, January 1999.

5. Comprising the governments of Britain, Canada, France, Germany, Italy, Japan and the USA.

6. In fact it may be regarded as not entirely a coincidence that this law was passed in the same year as the first major stock market collapse since funded pension schemes had become widely established in the United States. It should, moreover, be noted that the Pension Benefit Guaranty Corporation, set up under the Act to insure fund members' pension rights in the event of fund failure, did not produce a surplus in its first twenty years of operation, indicating the inadequacy of the premiums paid to cover the risks of insolvency. See Shutt, *The Trouble with Capitalism*, ch. 8.

7. As reflected in the benchmark Standard & Poor's 500 index of the US market – see Table 2.1.

8. It is true that such reluctance may also have been a function of the proportionately much bigger scale of losses. By 1999 Japanese government officials privately conceded that non-performing loans may have reached the equivalent of around $800 billion (some 20 per cent of GDP) – a reality that both the government and the banks themselves were long anxious to conceal (often with the help of blue-chip Western banks such as Credit Suisse First Boston in illegally 'window dressing' their accounts). See Gillian Tett, 'The Hidden Truth behind the Mask', *Financial Times*, 18 June 1999.

9. This was achieved by encouraging banks to buy large quantities of such Treasury stock just before the Federal Reserve lowered official interest rates, thereby precipitating a sharp rise in the prices of the bonds the banks had just bought – see Doug Noland, 'Credit Bubble Bulletin', 15 August 2003, www.prudentbear.com.

10. Bank for International Settlements, *Annual Report 1993*, Basel, June 1993.

11. Francis Fukuyama, *The End of History and the Last Man*, Hamish Hamilton, London, 1992,

12. Including one of the most high-profile financiers and speculators of the period, George Soros, in his book *The Crisis of Global Capitalism*, Macmillan, London, 1998.

13. Source: OECD.

14. See pp. 104–5.

15. Based on OECD data.

16. John Plender, *Going off the Rails: Global Capital and the Crisis of Legitimacy*, John Wiley, Chichester, 2003.

Chapter 2

1. In the case of the US benchmark S&P 500 index.

2. See Shutt, *The Trouble with Capitalism*, chs 6 and 8.

3. Ibid., ch. 5.

4. Ibid., chs 3 and 8.

5. But see Shutt, *The Trouble with Capitalism*, p. 124.

6. Such historically low pay-outs are only partly explained by the fact that by the 1990s it had become more 'tax-efficient' to return money to shareholders via buy-backs.

7. Particularly as the impossibility of sustaining double-digit earnings growth rates against a background of long-term annual GDP growth of 2–3 per cent was being constantly pointed out by leading financial journalists – see Barry Riley, 'Virtual Reality Answers', *Financial Times*, 29 July 1998 – in contrast to the bullish hype emanating from most of the media.

8. Although the USA and some other industrialised countries did experience actual falls in GDP, the overall performance of the OECD (including still strong growth in Japan and South Korea) meant that recession was technically avoided in the industrial market economies as a whole.

9. See Shutt, *The Trouble with Capitalism*, chs 4 and 7.

10. Ibid., pp. 101–2.

11. M. Blair and T. Kochan, *The New Relationship: Human Capital and the American Corporation*, Brookings Institution, Washington DC, 2002; quoted by James DeLong in *The Stock Options Controversy and the New*

Economy, Competitive Enterprise Institute, Washington DC, 2002.

12. See Shutt, *The Trouble with Capitalism*, ch. 7.

13. 'More Upheaval for the Restless Revolutionary', *Financial Times*, 28 October 2003.

14. Richard Tomkins, 'The Folly of Treating Children as Consumers', *Financial Times*, 28 November 2002.

15. Jon Silverman and David Wilson, *Innocence Betrayed: Paedophiles, the Media and Society*, Polity Press, Cambridge, 2003.

Chapter 3

1. The United States also moved temporarily into budget surplus at the end of the 1990s (for the first time in thirty years), although Japan moved even deeper into debt in a vain effort to escape from its decline into chronic stagnation.

2. Gerald Holtham 'Why the State Needs to Borrow More, Not Less, *Guardian*, 16 August 1999.

3. 'Bond Policy Costs UK £3bn a Year', *Financial Times*, 13 October 1999.

4. See Shutt, *The Trouble with Capitalism*, p. 12.

5. See ibid., p. 122.

6. See ibid., pp. 119–20; John Plender, *Going Off the Rails: Global Capital and the Crisis of Legitimacy*, John Wiley, Chichester, 2003.

7. Source: Bank for International Settlements.

8. Peter Drucker, quoted in Warren Buffett's annual letter to the shareholders of Berkshire Hathaway Inc., 1995.

9. Andrew Hill and Dan Roberts, 'GE Must Hone Predatory Instincts to Ensure Survival', *Financial Times*, 21 June 2002.

10. 'Tearing Down the Walls in Telecom', *Business Week*, 2 March 2004.

11. A vivid picture of the effect of such tactics in the dissipation of the assets of Marconi plc in Britain in 1999–2000 was given by the BBC *Money Programme* in 'The Men Who Broke Marconi', 14 November 2002.

12. The ironic term coined by Tom Wolfe to refer to overpaid Wall Street bond dealers in his masterly 1980s' satire, *The Bonfire of the Vanities*.

13. Geoff Dyer, 'Biotechnology Industry "Facing Funding Crisis"', *Financial Times*, 17 November 2003.

14. Mark Williams of Boston University, quoted in Sheila McNulty, 'Long Shadow of Enron Clouds Energy Traders', *Financial Times*, 18 February 2003.

15. Ibid.

16. Julie Earle, 'Shell's Gas-powered Fantasy', *Financial Times*, 15 July 2002.

Chapter 4

1. See Bank of International Settlements, *Annual Report 2003*.

2. See Shutt, *The Trouble with Capitalism*, pp. 78–81.

3. Warren Buffett, 'Who Really Cooks the Books?', *New York Times*, 24 July 2002.

4. Norma Cohen, 'How They Overlooked Longevity', *Financial Times*, Management Supplement, 9 February 2004.

5. Barry Riley, 'Reinventing Equities', *Financial Times*, 8–9 January 2000

6. See P. Krugman, 'A System Corrupted', *New York Times*, 18 January 2002.

7. 'UK Venture Capital Calls for Extra Tax Breaks', *Financial Times*, 25 November 2002. The contradictions implicit in this demand have been exposed by the recognition by a venture capitalist (writing in the same newspaper a year later) of the potential damage such subsidies can do to the industry – see Wim Borgdorff, 'Public Money Is Harming The VC Industry', *FTfm*, 16 February 2004.

8. E.g. the switch by the Reagan administration of the federal employees' pension scheme to funding from 1985 and the moves by successive British governments to phase out the State Earnings Related Pension Scheme from the early 1990s.

9. 'US Healthcare Fraud Convictions Rise', *Financial Times*, 11 August 2003. Although this report indicates that the Department of Justice had since 2000 begun to recover billions of dollars dishonestly obtained from the miscreant companies, it also shows that in many instances the offenders are allowed simply to reimburse the money without admitting wrongdoing – or even being excluded from

further participation in the programme – suggesting there is limited resolve on the part of the authorities to deter further wrongdoing.

10. 'Carillion Plans to Sell PFI Equity Stake', *Financial Times*, 11 September 2003.

11. Edmund McCarthy, 'Amazing Times', www.prudentbear.com, 18 July 2003.

12. See S. Pirani and E. Farrell, 'Western Financial Institutions and Russian Capitalism', paper delivered at academic conference on 'The World Crisis of Capitalism and the Post-Soviet States', Moscow 30 October–1 November 1999.

13. S. Fischer and A. Gelb, 'Issues in the Reform of Socialist Economies', in V. Corbo, F. Coricelli and J. Bossak, eds, *Reforming Central and Eastern European Economies: Initial Results and Challenges. A World Bank Symposium*, World Bank, Washington DC, September 1991.

14. J. Stiglitz, *Whither Reform? Ten Years of the Transition*, World Bank, Washington DC, April 1999.

15. BBC *Money Programme*, 29 October 2003 and 11 February 2004.

16. 'Parmalat's "30-year" Hole', *Financial Times*, 20 February 2004.

17. John Plender, *Going off the Rails: Global Capital and the Crisis of Legitimacy*, John Wiley, Chichester, 2003.

18. See Shutt, *The Trouble with Capitalism*, pp. 170–71.

19. 'Tax Avoiders Rob Wealth of Nations', *Observer*, 17 November 2002.

Chapter 5

1. Bank of International Settlements, *Annual Report 2003*.

2. Adam Smith, *The Wealth of Nations*, Book V, ch. 1.

3. In fact an authoritative study of the effects of such a regulation already in place for several years in Italy has indicated that the net effect of such requirement on the quality and independence of audits is minimal. See 'Rotation of Auditors "Has No Impact"', *Financial Times*, 17 September 2002.

4. They were re-emphasised in the seminal work of A.A. Berle and G.C. Means, *The Modern Corporation and Private Property*, Macmillan, New York, 1932.

5. Quoted in *Financial Times*, Fund Management supplement, 16 June 2003.

6. Reduced from five since Andersen was driven out of business by the Enron debacle.

7. Heather Connon, 'Independent Auditing? In Your Dreams', *Observer*, 9 February 2003.

8. 'EBITDA's Foggy Bottom Line', *Business Week*, 14 January 2003; 'Top 10 Limitations of EBITDA' developed by Moody's Investors Service, www.fleetcapital.com, February 2001.

9. *Financial Times*, 24 July 2003.

10. 'Wall Street "Barbarians" at Sainsbury's Gate', *Observer*, 4 April 2004.

11. 'Enron's Bankers: A Great Prison Escape', *Business Week*, 31 July 2003.

12. See Shutt, *The Trouble with Capitalism*, pp. 176–7; R. Monks and N. Minow, *Corporate Governance*, Blackwell, Oxford, 1996.

13. See Matthew Lynn, 'New Analyst Restrictions May Drive Investors Away', *Bloomberg News*, 29 September 2003.

Chapter 6

1. See Shutt, *The Trouble with Capitalism*, p. 212.

2. Kurt Richebacher, 'America's Recovery Is Not What It Seems', *Financial Times*, 5 September 2003. See also Shutt, *The Trouble with Capitalism*, pp. 194–5.

3. Indeed it seems likely that the huge fraudulent overstatements of corporate sales and value added which were later found to have occurred during the period also contributed significantly to the inflation of official US GDP statistics.

4. John Astin, *Quality Adjustment in CPIs – A Personal View*, Eurostat, Luxembourg, 1998.

5. This approach to measuring inflation, which has been used in the USA since the late 1960s, has since the late 1990s spread to Japan and Western Europe.

6. See OECD, *Disability Programmes in Need of Reform*, OECD, Paris, March 2003.

7. Source: IMF, *World Economic Outlook*, Washington DC, September 2003.

8. Speech to the European Parliament, 29 January 2004.

9. See P. Mullan, *The Imaginary Time Bomb*, I.B. Tauris, London, 2000.

10. For an honourable exception, see Will Hutton, 'The Great Pensions Lie', *Observer*, 16 February 2003.

11. See, e.g., 'Work Longer, Have More Babies', *The Economist*, 25 September 2003.

12. The term used by Alan Greenspan, Chairman of the US Federal Reserve Board, in 1996 to draw attention to the already serious over-valuation of the stock market – which was nevertheless to double again before the crash.

13. Marshall Auerback, 'China: The New Fulcrum of the Global Economy?', www.prudentbear.com, 30 December 2003.

14. 'Merger Mania?', *Financial Times*, 29 October 2003.

15. Notably in the case of the takeover of FleetBoston Financial by Bank of America announced in October 2003.

16. 'The US International Investment Position at Year-End 2001', *Capital Flows Monitor*, Financial Markets Center, Philomont VA, 26 July 2002.

17. See, for example, the weekly *Credit Bubble Bulletin* by Doug Noland, published by David W. Tice & Associates, www.prudentbear.com.

18. To use the famous phrase coined by one of their number, J.A. Schumpeter, to define what he considered to be the benign capitalist dynamic.

19. See Shutt, *The Trouble with Capitalism*, pp. 60–61.

20. *Christian Science Monitor*, 27 December 2002.

21. See an account of the Enron scandal, 'More Crime Syndicate than Energy Company', *Financial Times*, 20 Febrary 2004.

22. Among the many accounts of this affair available on the Internet (but never mentioned in the mainstream media) are 'The Bush Family and the Savings and Loan Scandal', la.indymedia.org, 6 January 2004.

23. Harry Shutt, *A New Democracy: Alternatives to a Bankrupt World Order*, Zed Books, London, 2001, p. 61; *Financial Times*, 1 June 2001.

24. See Shutt, *The Trouble with Capitalism*, ch. 11.

Chapter 7

1. 'The West Knows Now There Is No Wall to Hide Behind', *Guardian*, 13 November 2001.

2. See Shutt, *A New Democracy*, chs 3 and 4.

3. Estimates derived from US Department of Commerce, Bureau of Economic Analysis, *National Income and Product Accounts*; and National Statistics Office, UK National Accounts, *The Blue Book 2003*, HMSO, London, 2003.

4. Their conspicuous role in disrupting the World Trade Organisation summit in Seattle in 1999 marks their first appearance on the world stage.

5. See Shutt, *The Trouble with Capitalism*, chs 9 and 10.

6. E.g. Philip Bobbitt, *The Shield of Achilles: War, Peace and the Course of History*, Allen Lane, London, 2003; Robert Cooper, 'The New Liberal Imperialism', *Observer*, 7 April 2002.

Index